COUNSELING WITH OUR COUNCILS

LEARNING TO MINISTER TOGETHER

IN THE CHURCH AND

IN THE FAMILY

M. RUSSELL BALLARD

Deseret Book Company
Salt Lake City, Utah

Library of Congress Cataloging-in-Publication Data
  Ballard, M. Russell, 1928–
    Counseling with our councils : learning to minister together in
  the church and in the family / M. Russell Ballard.
        p.   cm.
    Includes bibliographical references and index.
    ISBN 1-57345-209-2 (hardcover)
    1. Church of Jesus Christ of Latter-day Saints—Government.
  2. Mormon Church—Government.   3. Church group work.   4. Local
  church councils.   5. Women in the Mormon Church.   6. Church growth.
  I. Title.
  BX8657.B35   1997
  262'.09332—dc21   97-38121
                                                                 CIP

Printed in the United States of America   72076-2980
Publishers Printing, Salt Lake City, UT

10   9   8

CONTENTS

PREFACE

The world in which we are now living is filled with things that are in direct opposition to the teachings of the Lord Jesus Christ. Great pressures from Satan are evident all around us. Our families are under attack, and our youth are being bombarded with evil influences. Over the last few decades we have been blessed with marvelous technological advances of all kinds, but during the same period we have seen dramatic increases in immorality, abortion, divorce, child abuse, drug abuse, violent crime, and many other social ills.

Of special concern is the effect these trends have had on the family. For example, one social commentator has written that "the present illegitimacy ratio is not only unprecedented in the past two centuries; it is unprecedented, so far as we know, in American history going back to colonial times, and in English history from Tudor times" (Himmelfarb, *De-Moralization of Society*, 23). And a noted family historian at Princeton University, Lawrence Stone, has said: "The scale of marital breakdowns in the West since 1960 has no historical precedent that I know of, and seems unique. . . . There has been nothing like it for the last 2,000 years, and probably longer" (quoted in Popenoe, "World without Fathers," 13).

Circumstances are so different today from when I was a teenager, a young bishop, and even a bishop for the second time. As President Ezra Taft Benson testified, "Wickedness is rapidly expanding in every segment of our society. . . . It is more highly organized, more cleverly disguised, and more powerfully promoted than ever before" ("I Testify," 87).

Because of these conditions, I have had on my mind for several years now the question: How can the Church best prepare all of its members to cope with today's challenges and ever-changing circumstances?

No longer can any one leader, either man or woman—or for that matter, any parent—attempt to provide what is so desperately needed in the lives of our families and Church members. If we are to succeed in leading our Heavenly Father's children toward eternal life, we must counsel together and help each other.

My thoughts go frequently to the inspired council system that exists in the Church. It is clear to me that the Lord has provided us with a sound tool to help us minister more effectively to our people and solve the problems that confront individuals and families.

We each bear the primary responsibility for meeting our own spiritual and temporal needs, and most of us can turn to immediate and extended family members for assistance, counsel, and encouragement. But the Lord has also established, both in the Church and in our homes, a system of councils designed to strengthen and uplift every Latter-day Saint. These range from the Council of the First Presidency and the Quorum of the Twelve Apostles to the family council, and all play an important role in blessing and saving souls. Within the Church, much of this sacred work is accomplished at the stake and ward levels. (Throughout this book, the terms *stake* and *ward* also apply to *district* and *branch*.)

Many of our bishops and stake presidents are burdened with the personal problems of the Church members for whom they have stewardship. Every resource available must be enlisted to win the battle for the souls of our Father's children. I feel strongly that the best way to help lift the burden is to invite stake and ward council members to assist in finding the answers and implementing the solutions that the gospel of Jesus Christ provides. Pages at the end of this book may be used for writing down ideas for finding those answers and then implementing the solutions.

It would be well in appropriate instances to include auxiliary leaders in the discussions aimed at finding wise solutions to our many challenges. Sister leaders are members of stake and ward councils as well as stake and ward welfare committees. Priesthood leaders cannot afford to overlook the experience, wisdom, sensitivity, and insight women bring to such deliberations. One of my main purposes in writing this book is to encourage priesthood leaders to invite the sisters to more fully participate in developing solutions to the difficult problems confronting members of the Church.

Our leaders have provided clear statements that help us better understand the vital contribution sisters can make to the gospel kingdom. Consider this plea from President Howard W. Hunter: "It seems to me that there is a great need to rally the women of the Church to stand with and for the Brethren in stemming the tide of evil that surrounds us and in moving forward the work of our Savior. . . . Obedient to him we are a majority. But only together can we accomplish the work he has given us to do and be prepared for the day when we shall see him" ("To the Women of the Church," 96).

My sincere desire is that this book will help all those who have been called to lead and serve in the gospel kingdom gain a wider vision of the power that exists in the councils that have been put in place in The Church of Jesus Christ of Latter-day Saints.

ACKNOWLEDGMENTS

I am indebted to a number of people who have contributed to the development of this book. My secretary, Carolyn Hyde, has been immensely helpful in doing research and in preparing and revising the manuscript. Several friends and colleagues have read drafts of the manuscript and have offered insightful recommendations for improvement. Consultation and assistance from Joseph Walker and Andrew Allison have helped me move the work forward. Ron Millett and Sheri Dew at Deseret Book have encouraged this project from its earliest stages, and other members of the Deseret Book team, including Kent Ware, Suzanne Brady, Richard Erickson, and Tonya Facemyer, have helped convert the manuscript into a finished publication. As always, I express my love and appreciation to my wife, Barbara, for her patience and constant encouragement. Notwithstanding the excellent contributions and suggestions of these and many other people, I alone bear responsibility for what is written in this book.

SPIRITUAL SYNERGISM

In my introduction to the book *Our Search for Happiness,* I asked readers to consider for a moment the word *understanding.* "It's a simple word, really—one that most of us use every day," I wrote. "But it means something that is quite remarkable. With understanding we can strengthen relationships, revitalize neighborhoods, unify nations, and even bring peace to a troubled world. Without it chaos, intolerance, hate, and war are often the result.

"In other words, *mis*understanding" (Ballard, *Our Search for Happiness,* 1).

As with that previous volume, my primary objective in writing this book is to facilitate understanding. In this case, I'm writing primarily to Church members who have been called to serve on one of the many different kinds of councils that exist in the Church, such as stake presidencies, bishoprics, ward and stake councils, and auxiliary presidencies. In addition, many adult members preside over family councils. It is my sincere hope that those who read these pages will have a better sense of what a Church council is, how it should function, and how members can magnify their contribution to the process of counseling through our councils.

In other words, *understanding.*

Several years ago I was assigned to attend a stake conference in Europe. When I arrived at the stake center, I met the stake Relief Society president, who was busy preparing some refreshments for the stake presidency and me. I took occasion to visit with her privately to thank her for her faithful service. While we were talking, I asked her how she was feeling about her calling in the Church.

"Elder Ballard," she said, her voice edged with exasperation, "will the brethren of the Church ever understand that the sisters want to make a contribution to the real issues facing the Church and its members?"

As you might expect, I was a little surprised at her answer and the palpable frustration that clearly had prompted it. So I asked her to elaborate.

"Sometimes I feel like the hired help at the council table," she said. "I'm there to serve, but not to contribute. When they talk about ways to accomplish the mission of the Church, my opinion is never sought, and when they refer to the decisions of stake leaders, they never acknowledge me as a leader who can make a contribution to the spiritual growth and development of stake members. Sometimes they even talk about ways to meet the needs of the sisters in our stake without inviting me to participate. I'm given assignments, and I do what I'm told. But I never feel that I am asked to *counsel*. Is that the way it's supposed to work?"

My first thought was: "How can this be? She is a member of the stake council and the leader of the Relief Society in her stake. How can she feel that she is not a part of things?" I assured her that it was not the Lord's program to ignore the magnificent spiritual capabilities of those who have been called through inspiration to preside over stake and ward Relief Society, Young Women, and Primary organizations. Indeed, God has inspired the creation of a council system that is intended to harness the insight and experience of all who have been called to serve in key leadership positions in the ward and stake. But my conversation with this good sister made me wonder: How many of our Relief Society presidents feel that way? How many Primary presidents? How many Young Women presidents? How many of our elders quorum presidents, high priests group leaders, high councilors, and other organizational leaders feel unrepresented around the council table or within the ward or stake community they serve? How well do we understand the council system? Do we appreciate the power, vitality, and strength it can add to our respective ministries among God's children in these latter days?

This experience and others like it prompted me to address the subject in general conference. In fact, for two consecutive general conferences I stood at the pulpit in the Salt Lake Tabernacle on Temple Square and spoke about the importance of the council system in The Church of Jesus Christ of Latter-day Saints. I attempted to teach about the great spiritual power and inspired direction that come from properly conducted family, ward, and stake councils. I promised parents that their families will be greatly blessed if they will counsel with one another. I also promised ward and stake leaders that their service will be more effective if they will learn to harness the collective wisdom, experience, faith, and testimony of all the members of Church councils.

After my first conference address on the subject, I was anxious to learn whether my remarks had been understood, particularly by our wonderful bishops. Perhaps it's just my business background, but I'm always anxious to see results. So during training sessions I conducted in various locations around the world, I focused a great deal of attention on the ward council. As part of the training I would assemble a simulated ward council from among those attending the meeting. A bishop in attendance was assigned to lead the council, and to him I would give a theoretical problem involving a less-active family. I then asked the bishop to use the ward council to develop a plan to activate this family.

Without exception, the "bishop" would take charge of the situation and say, "Here's the problem, and here's what I think we should do to solve it." Then he would make assignments to the respective ward council members. This was a good exercise in delegation, I suppose, but it didn't even begin to utilize the experience and wisdom of council members in addressing the problem. Eventually I would suggest to the bishop that he try again, only this time asking for some ideas and recommendations from the members of his council before making any decisions. I especially encouraged him to ask the sisters for their ideas. I tried to teach the concept that although men and women shoulder different responsibilities, they bring to their Church service varying backgrounds, talents, experiences, and points of view. It is no secret that men and women tend to see things from their own unique perspectives—both of which are equally valid and equally useful and necessary in the work of our councils. Not coincidentally, when the bishop opened up the meeting and invited council members to counsel together during the training session, it was like opening the floodgates of heaven: a reservoir of insight and inspiration suddenly began to flow between council members as they planned for the fellowshipping of a less active family.

As I watched this same scenario played out before me time after time, I decided that it would not be out of order for me to write in some detail about the importance of councils, because there is a great need in the Church for leaders, particularly stake presidents, bishops, and parents, to understand and harvest the spiritual power of the council system. There is no problem in the family, ward, or stake that cannot be solved if we look for solutions in the Lord's way by counseling—really counseling—with one another.

Before we proceed, however, it would probably be helpful if

we take a moment to consider a definition of the word *council,* just to be sure we're approaching the subject from the same perspective. After all, if you look up the word in an unabridged dictionary, you will find many definitions. For the purposes of our discussion, however, I would like to offer this succinct definition of Church councils from an article in the *Encyclopedia of Mormonism:*

> The concept of a council in The Church of Jesus Christ of Latter-day Saints embodies both a philosophy of administrative behavior and an organizational body or unit. There are formally constituted councils, such as the Council of [the] Twelve Apostles, . . . stake high councils, and councils consisting of priesthood quorum and auxiliary officers who work together as ward councils or stake councils. To these councils concerned representatives (athletic, single adult, etc.) are sometimes added. Church councils coordinate and schedule activities, gather information, plan future programs or events, and make decisions and resolve problems for their units. . . .
>
> The philosophy of a council is what sociologist Thomas O'Dea called a "democracy of participation" in Mormon culture (*The Mormons* [Chicago, 1964], p. 165). At periodic council meetings both individual and organizational needs are considered. Recognizing the unique circumstances surrounding a particular unit, geographical area, or set of individuals, the council identifies the programs and activities that need to be planned and correlated. (The council does not have final decision-making power; this resides with the unit leader, such as the stake president or bishop.)
>
> Councils are more than operational coordinating mechanisms. They also serve as vehicles for family, ward, stake, region, area, or general Church teaching

and development. As members participate in councils, they learn about larger organizational issues. They see leadership in action, learning how to plan, analyze problems, make decisions, and coordinate across subunit boundaries. Participation in councils helps prepare members for future leadership responsibilities. ("Priesthood Councils," in Ludlow, *Encyclopedia of Mormonism*, 3:1141–42)

I believe that the day has come when we cannot hope to build the Church and to bring the hearts and souls of our members to Christ without using every resource the Lord has given us to help us take advantage of our opportunities and address the obstacles standing in our way. For example, leaders throughout the Church are greatly concerned about the spiritual maturity of many members. We worry about the inactivity of so many new members of the Church. I believe that the answer to these concerns lies in the proper understanding and use of our councils, particularly the ward council. Is it too much to believe that the bishops and branch presidents of the Church can harness their collective resources and stop this unnecessary loss of so many of our Heavenly Father's children?

If the ward mission leader understood that the auxiliaries are a resource to assist in missionary work, he could suggest to the Relief Society presidency that they visit the home of an investigator family during the time that the missionaries are teaching them the discussions and invite the mother of the family to attend a Relief Society activity or meeting. No extra meetings are required—just an alert ward mission leader who wants to enlist the help of the ward council to work with the missionaries in fellowshipping a family into the Church. Similarly, Young Men, Young Women, and Primary leaders could get involved with members of the family who fall within their respective areas of responsibility. Can you see how comfortable and appropriate it would be to launch a fellowshipping process that could contribute to the conversion and retention of any man, woman, teenager, or child who is investigating the Church? If in council meetings each council member is concerned about supporting the missionaries, I believe many more of our converts would be fully fellowshipped into the Church.

The same concept applies to almost any concern facing a branch, ward, stake, or family. For example, we worry about the less-active members of the Church. We spend many hours in various meetings talking about them and planning how we can bless their lives. Can you see the potential power of the priesthood and auxiliaries working together to systematically reach out to families and individuals? I believe that the answers to the activity problems facing our wards and stakes can be found in the priesthood and auxiliary councils. I also believe that Satan does not want us to figure out how to effectively use the council system.

The Brethren have worried for years about the heavy load our bishops and branch presidents carry. To me, the very best way for them to ease some of their burden is to counsel with their councils.

For most of my life before I was called as a General Authority of The Church of Jesus Christ of Latter-day Saints, I was involved in the automobile business, as was my father before me. Through the years I learned to appreciate the sound and performance of a well-tuned engine. As far as I'm concerned, it's almost musical—from the gentle purring of an idling motor to the vibrant roar of a throttle fully open. And the power that sound represents is even more exciting. There's nothing quite like sitting behind the wheel of a fine automobile when all of the pistons are firing as they should and all of the assembled parts are pulling together.

On the other hand, there's nothing more exasperating than a car that isn't functioning properly. No matter how beautifully it is painted or how comfortably it is furnished inside, a car with an engine that isn't fully functional is just a shell of unrealized potential. While it is possible for an automobile to run on only a few cylinders, it will never go as far or as fast, nor will the ride be as smooth and pleasant, as when it is properly tuned. And when a few cylinders carry a load designed to be borne by more, the quality of performance deteriorates.

Unfortunately, there are too many stakes, wards, and families in the Church that are hitting on only a few cylinders—including some that are trying to make do with only one. The one-cylinder ward is one in which the bishop handles all the problems, makes all the decisions, follows through on all the assignments, and faces every challenge. Then, like any other overworked cylinder, he starts to sputter and behave erratically. Eventually, he burns out altogether.

I remember speaking to a young bishop one day. As he lovingly spoke of his ministry, he shared one overwhelming anxiety. "The biggest frustration," he said, "is that there just isn't enough time in the day to do everything that needs to be done."

How well I remembered that feeling from my own days as a bishop. So I tried to keep a straight face as I said, "You know, I think you're the first bishop in the entire history of the Church who's ever felt that way!"

Obviously, the demands upon our bishops are great. There are certain priesthood keys that they—and they alone—hold, and certain roles in the ward that only they can fulfill. But they are not called to be all things to all people. They are called to preside and to lead and to extend God's love to His children. But no one, least of all our Heavenly Father, expects them to do it all themselves.

The same can be said of our stake presidents, quorum presidents, auxiliary presidents, and mothers and fathers in their families. All face responsibilities that require much of their time, talent, and energy. But none are left to do it alone. God, the

Master Organizer, has inspired the creation of a system of committees and councils. If understood and carefully implemented and utilized, that system will lessen the burden on any one individual leader and extend the reach and impact of his or her ministry by bringing together the judgment, talents, and wisdom of many leaders who are entitled to the guidance and inspiration of the Holy Spirit. The council system also acts as a safeguard to the Church, providing support and strength where individual leaders may be weak.

As a member of the Quorum of the Twelve Apostles, I serve on a number of general Church councils and committees. It is one of the great blessings of my life to work and serve with dedicated men and women whose greatest wish is to do their Heavenly Father's will. We have had some marvelous experiences as we have counseled together, sometimes for hours at a time, formulating plans, programs, and policies to bless and strengthen the entire membership of the Church during these difficult and challenging times.

Although I consider such service a rare and wonderful opportunity, I don't mind telling you that our task isn't always as easy as it may sound. With the rich diversity of languages, cultures, and environments that currently exist within the Church, all of our planning and preparation on a general level has to be both broad and narrow: broad enough to meet the varying needs of millions of members in dozens of different nations, and narrow enough to reach the one. To this end, priesthood and auxiliary leaders regularly seek the Lord on bended knee and plead for His guidance and direction. And we have been edified and uplifted by the spirit of inspiration—and yes, revelation—as it has come.

In many ways, our general Church councils function much the same as local Church and family councils should function. Under the direction of the priesthood and the influence of the Holy Spirit, these councils should feature free and open discussion and clear, concise communication. Our mutual goals and objectives should always be clearly understood. Everything we do, everything we teach, every plan we make should be focused on helping God's children enjoy the full blessings of the gospel. In this effort, councils should support families, striving never to be in competition with them.

Therefore, our council meetings are about duties and responsibilities, not turf. They provide an opportunity for the priesthood quorums and auxiliary organizations of the Church to come together in a spirit of loving cooperation to assist Heavenly Father in accomplishing His very work and glory: "to bring to pass the immortality and eternal life of man" (Moses 1:39). The same is true of our family councils, only there it is a matter of parents and children joining forces in an energetic and dynamic way to ensure that there are no empty places at our eternal family tables.

And if ever there was a time when such cooperative effort between family members and the men and women leaders in the Church was needed in behalf of Heavenly Father's children, this is the time. These are perilous days, and they require absolute vigilance on the part of all who have been entrusted with watch care in the kingdom. Our individual responsibilities are great, but just as important is the responsibility we share with others at home and in the Church to come together in a united effort to bless the lives of our family members and all of our eternal brothers and sisters.

SPIRITUAL SYNERGISM

Scientists call this process *synergism*, defined as a "united action of different agents or organisms producing a greater effect than the sum of the various individual actions" (*Thorndike-Barnhardt Dictionary*, s.v. "synergism"). The ancient moralist Aesop used to illustrate the concept by holding up a stick and asking for a volunteer among his listeners who thought he could break it. Of course the volunteer was able to break the stick easily. Then Aesop would put two sticks of the same size together and would ask the same volunteer to break them both at the same time. It was more difficult, but usually it could be done without too much trouble. The process was repeated, with another stick being added to the bundle each time, until the volunteer was unable to break the bundle of sticks. The moral to Aesop's illustration was simple: individually we are weak, but together we are strong.

It has never been God's intention that His children stand alone in important decisions and responsibilities. During our premortal existence, He himself called for a grand council to present His glorious plan for our eternal welfare. His Church is organized with councils at every level, beginning with the Council of the First Presidency and the Quorum of the Twelve Apostles and extending right on through to our stake, ward, and family councils. The Apostle Paul taught that the organization of the Church, complete with apostles, prophets, and other officers and teachers, was given by the Savior "for the perfecting of the saints, for the work of the ministry, for the edifying of the body of Christ: till we all come in the unity of the faith" (Ephesians 4:11–13).

In his first letter to the Corinthian Saints, Paul compared the members of the Church and their various responsibilities to the operation of the physical body:

> For the body is not one member, but many. . . .
> But now hath God set the members every one of them in the body, as it hath pleased him.
> And if they were all one member, where were the body?
> But now are they many members, yet but one body.
> And the eye cannot say unto the hand, I have no

need of thee: nor again the head to the feet, I have no need of you. . . .

That there should be no schism in the body; but that the members should have the same care one for another.

And whether one member suffer, all the members suffer with it; or one member be honoured, all the members rejoice with it. (1 Corinthians 12:14, 18–21, 25–26)

The scriptures make it clear that though our respective roles may be different and may change from time to time, all are equally important to the successful functioning of the Church. We need the priesthood quorums to assert themselves and fulfill their divinely mandated responsibilities, just as we need the Relief Society, the Primary, the Young Women, the Sunday School, and the activities committees to perform their vital functions. And we need all of those inspired organizations to work together in council, assisting each other as needed, for the benefit of individuals and families.

Just a few years ago, Sherry, a single mother of two beautiful daughters, moved into a new ward. It had been a long time since she had been active in the Church, but lately she had been feeling some strong spiritual yearnings. So she was pleased when the elders quorum presidency showed up to help her move in, and she accepted their invitation to attend a quorum social later in the week.

The very next night the Relief Society presidency dropped in, followed by one daughter's Young Women adviser and the other daughter's Primary teacher. By the time the bishopric got there later in the evening, Sherry was feeling like she already knew everyone in the ward. Each visit had been warm and friendly, and by the time Sunday rolled around Sherry and her daughters were ready and eager to attend Church.

"None of these people had ever met me before," Sherry said later, "and yet they made me feel like I was coming home."

And in a very real way, she was. The outpouring of affection and interest gave her the courage she needed to make significant changes in her life. Within a week she had a calling in the ward, and her daughters were involved in their respective class activities and projects.

As Sherry embraced her new ward and was welcomed and accepted by the members there, she became open and receptive to the Spirit of the Lord as it moved upon her. Her testimony was revitalized and her faith restored. A little more than a year after she moved into the ward, many of her new friends and neighbors joined her in the temple, where she made sacred covenants that she is faithfully keeping to this day.

Not too long ago I had a chance to talk with Sherry's bishop about the experience. "I wish I could tell you that it always happens that way," he told me. "Sometimes things work out better than at other times. But when the entire program of the Church comes together in council like that to focus on the specific needs of one family or individual, miracles can and do happen."

It is my testimony that such miracles can happen only to the extent that we are prepared to work together—the men and women who serve in the quorums and auxiliaries of the Church—to make them happen. This is not men's work or women's work in which we are involved; it is all God's work. We are on His errand, and we serve at His will and pleasure.

President Ezra Taft Benson once said:

> There is a principle cited in the Doctrine and Covenants which, though directed specifically to the leading quorums of the Church, applies to all councils in Church government. I quote from section 107: . . . "The decisions of these quorums [or councils] . . . are to be made in all righteousness, in holiness, and lowliness of heart, meekness and long suffering, and in faith, and virtue, and knowledge, temperance, patience, godliness,

13

brotherly kindness and charity" [D&C 107:30]. . . . This seems to me to be the pattern by which the Lord would have us operate through priesthood councils at all levels of Church government. We must be one in all aspects of this work . . . for all things are spiritual to Him whom we acknowledge as Master. ("Church Government through Councils," 88–89)

It has been my experience that where leaders make wise use of committees and councils, lives are blessed. Like a carefully manufactured automobile operating at peak efficiency, such Church organizations move the work of the Lord faster and farther. They are unified, and together they experience a much more pleasant ride along the highway of Church service.

One important way to increase the unity and effectiveness of our ward and stake councils is to remember that all council members have a dual responsibility: not only do they represent the needs and perspectives of the individual organizations they have been called to lead, but each one also serves as a member of the *council,* sharing equally with the others a sense of stewardship for the success of the Lord's work in that area. Thus when a subject that pertains to all ward or stake members is discussed, full consideration should be given to the views and recommendations of all council members, both the brethren and the sisters. Such an approach will result in wiser decisions and will generate greater commitment as these decisions are carried out.

When Church leaders allow those whom the Lord has called to serve with them to become part of a problem-solving team, wonderful things begin to happen. We broaden our base of experience and understanding, which can't help but expose us to better and more insightful solutions. We energize individuals by giving them a chance to have input and to be heard. We prepare future leaders by allowing them to participate and learn.

And when more people feel ownership of the problem, more people are willing to become part of the solution, which greatly enhances the possibility of success.

Once the appropriate councils are in place and energized, leaders can begin to look beyond maintenance and meeting the needs of individuals and can find ways to make the world a better place in which to live. There's no reason why ward council agendas could not include such subjects as gang violence, urban blight, unemployment, or abuse of any kind. Bishops could ask ward councils, "How can we make a difference in our community and in our families in these important areas?" Such broad thinking and involvement in our communities would not only be exciting and fulfilling; it would also have the benefit of being the right thing for us to do as Latter-day Saints and as Christians.

In other words, one of the great strengths of the council system is the flexibility it provides to develop and implement local solutions to local problems. And as the needs and circumstances of individuals, families, and communities change over time, ward and stake councils—operating under priesthood direction and established Church guidelines—can focus their collective wisdom and the inspiration of heaven on such needs, thus blessing and lifting all who come within their influence.

THE POWER OF COUNCILS

Throughout my years of service in the Church, I have seen extraordinary examples of the power of counseling with our councils. Some years ago when I was serving as a bishop, a large family in our ward experienced a crisis when the father lost his job. I was concerned about their well-being during this difficult time, and I visited their home to counsel with them and to offer the support and assistance of the Church. Interestingly, they were reluctant to respond to my offer of temporary assistance, and so I took the matter to my ward welfare committee and to the ward council. In a spirit of loving confidentiality, I shared with them my concern for this wonderful family and asked for their ideas as to how we could bless the lives of our brothers and sisters who lived in that home. Our Relief Society president volunteered to visit with the mother of the family to ascertain their temporal needs and to work with them in obtaining any commodities they needed—all of which, of course, was her responsibility according to the program of the Church. Within a couple of days, she was able to accomplish what I had been unable to accomplish, and the family humbly and gratefully accepted commodity assistance. The elders quorum president counseled with the father of the family—which, of course, was his right and duty—and worked with him on ways to improve his employment situation. Our Young Men president noticed that the family's house was in desperate need of a coat of paint, and he arranged for his priests to work with the high priests group to paint the house.

During the course of my conversations with the parents, I discovered that they were heavily in debt and were in arrears on their mortgage. Following approved welfare guidelines, I inquired about the ability of their extended family to help through this challenging period in their lives, but I received little information. Our Relief Society president, however, was able to learn that the mother had a brother who was very wealthy.

"There's no reason to contact him," the mother said. "We haven't even spoken in years. I can't go to him after all these years and say, 'Hi! Remember me? I'm your sister. Can you lend me some money?'"

I understood her dilemma, and yet I felt it was important to follow the order of the Church. And so I counseled with her and eventually received her permission to contact her brother, who lived in a distant city. I called him and explained the difficult circumstances in which his younger sister was living. Within three days he arrived in Salt Lake City and helped get his sister's financial affairs in order. Meanwhile, our elders quorum president was helping her husband to find a steady job with a good income. Suddenly, the family was more secure than they had ever been.

More important, however, was that they were closer and more united as a family. I don't think I'll ever forget that tender moment of reunion between the mother and her brother after years of estrangement. Although her brother had become alienated from the Church, there was an immediate spirit-to-spirit bonding that can be understood only from within a gospel context. So it probably won't surprise you to learn that as a result of this experience, the brother eventually returned to full activity in the Church and renewed his relationship with all of his living family members. And all of this happened because of the inspired work of a faithful ward council, functioning according to the program that God has outlined for His children through His servants.

Through years of such experiences, I have come to believe with all my heart that the council system of the Church has been divinely structured to bless the lives of our Heavenly Father's children. And to be perfectly candid, I sometimes have a difficult time understanding why so many of our leaders fail to see the vision of how working through councils can enhance their ability to accomplish all that the Lord expects of them in their respective stewardships.

For example, one great challenge facing the Church today is the need to fellowship and retain the ever-growing number of new converts. In some parts of the world, where the equivalent of a new ward is baptized every year, this is a truly daunting task. It would be difficult, if not impossible, for a bishop or branch president to even consider accomplishing this critical assignment without the ongoing efforts of hard-working councils in which the members are equally yoked together for the benefit of all of God's children in their ward or branch.

Similarly, the ward council that regularly discusses how the quorums and auxiliaries can provide fellowshipping opportunities for all who are investigating the Church will do much to cultivate a sense of belonging and compatibility throughout the ward. For example, if the Primary sisters would invite children who are prospective new members to attend Primary, these children would meet new friends and would feel that the Church really cares about them. Surely this would help the missionaries in the conversion of their families. All members of the council should watch for opportunities to give investigators a chance to develop a relationship with someone besides the missionaries. The ward mission leader can coordinate this work through the priesthood executive committee and directly with the leaders of the auxiliaries. Remember, the ward mission leader meets every week with the full-time missionaries to review the families they are teaching and to coordinate their work.

In a very real sense, the ward council is the "receiving arm" of the Church. If ward councils are functioning as they should, every new convert will be fellowshipped, will have home teachers and visiting teachers, and will receive an appropriate calling within days after baptism. Also, the less active will receive callings that assure them that they are needed and loved by the ward members.

Since 1985 I have served as a member of a council composed of twelve men. We come from different backgrounds, and we bring to the Quorum of the Twelve Apostles a diverse assortment of experiences in the Church and in the world. Be assured that in our meetings, we don't just sit around and wait for the President of our Quorum to tell us what to do. We counsel with each other, and we listen to each other with profound respect for the diverse abilities our Brethren bring to the Quorum. We discuss a wide variety of issues, from Church administration to world events, and we do so frankly and openly. Sometimes issues are discussed for weeks, months, and occasionally even years before a decision is made. We don't always agree during the initial course of our discussions. Once a decision is made, however, we are always united.

Of course, even in the Quorum of the Twelve Apostles, we never forget the important guiding principle of revelation through those who hold priesthood keys of leadership and authority. While counseling through councils is essential to successful gospel governance, those who serve in Church councils must be careful not to misunderstand their role in the process. The council is not a democratic forum. There are no veto overrides, and there is no majority rule. As necessary as council input is to the operation of Church units everywhere, it never supersedes the direction of the Holy Spirit as it manifests itself through revelation to those who hold priesthood keys.

President David O. McKay once told of a meeting of the Quorum of the Twelve Apostles in which a question of grave importance came up. He and the other Apostles felt strongly about a certain course of action that should be taken, and they were prepared to share their feelings in a meeting with the First Presidency later that morning. But to their surprise, President Joseph F. Smith didn't ask for their opinion in the matter, as was his custom. Rather, he arose and said, "'This is what the Lord wants.'

"While it was not wholly in harmony with what [we] had decided," President McKay wrote, "President Francis M. Lyman, the President of the Twelve, was the first on his feet to say, 'Brethren, I move that that becomes the opinion and judgment of this Council.'

"'Second the motion,' said another, and it was unanimous. Six months did not pass before the wisdom of that leader was demonstrated" (*Gospel Ideals,* 264).

Thank goodness for the principle of revelation in the Church! But let us not underestimate the worth of input from council members in the deliberation process. This is part of the miracle of Church councils. By listening to each other and to the Spirit, council members can advance the work of the Lord in meaningful ways. And as we support one another and participate in Church councils, we begin to understand how God can take ordinary men and women and make of them extraordinary leaders. For the best leaders are not those who work themselves to death trying to do everything single-handedly; the best leaders are those who follow God's plan and counsel with their councils.

The Lord said in an earlier dispensation through the prophet Isaiah, "Come now, and let us reason together" (Isaiah 1:18). And in this dispensation He repeated that admonition: "Let us reason together, that ye may understand" (D&C 50:10). This book will attempt to outline in some detail the Lord's plan for "reasoning together" through family, ward, and stake councils. We'll explore the doctrinal foundations of the council system, discuss the functions and purposes of a wide variety of councils, and offer some practical suggestions for council leaders and members. The world we now live in requires from members and leaders of the Church our very best thinking and the wisest use of every resource our Heavenly Father has given to us to build and protect His children and His Church.

All of the examples and experiences I will share are real, but I have chosen not to use any actual names or locations in order to protect the privacy of those who have shared their stories with me. Many of these real-life experiences have been submitted in writing to me by stake presidents, stake and ward auxiliary officers, bishops, and others who have seen firsthand the wonderful, positive power of counseling with our councils.

But before we get to those experiences, we'll take a look at the spiritual history of councils, beginning with a most important gathering—one that none of us can really remember—the great premortal Council in Heaven.

CHAPTER 1

THE GRAND COUNCIL

My maternal grandfather, Hyrum Mack Smith, was the eldest son of President Joseph F. Smith, the sixth President of the Church. When my grandfather unexpectedly died in 1918, just two months shy of his forty-sixth birthday, it was a great sadness to all who knew and loved him— including his father, the prophet. As any parent would feel anguish at the passing of a beloved child, President Smith spent a great deal of time in earnest prayer and spiritual contemplation, looking for comfort in the days that followed his son's death. Especially he pondered over God's eternal plan of salvation and its personal implications for each of us in this life and the next.

On October 3, 1918, just a few months after Hyrum's death, President Smith was sitting in his room "pondering over the scriptures" (D&C 138:1) when a marvelous vision was opened to him. President Smith was given the unique opportunity to look beyond the veil and see some of what transpired in the spirit world before this life as well as what will take place in the life that awaits us beyond this one.

What he learned during this incredible experience was extraordinary. For example, he was given to understand this significant concept regarding early Church leaders such as his father and uncle, Hyrum and Joseph Smith, as well as Brigham Young, John Taylor, Wilford Woodruff, and others: "Even before they were born, they, with many others, received their first lessons in the world of spirits and were prepared to come forth in the due time of the Lord to labor in his vineyard for the salvation of the souls of men" (D&C 138:56).

One of the key lessons Heavenly Father taught us in that "world of spirits" was the important role of councils and counseling together in gospel governance. From the very beginning, God has done His work through a system of organized councils.

The first council of which we are aware occurred before the world on which we live was created, in a place all of us have been but none of us can remember. God, our Heavenly Father, was the presiding authority at this most significant gathering. At His side was His firstborn, Jehovah, whom we now know as Jesus Christ. We don't know exactly how this Council in Heaven was conducted or the procedure that was followed. Although we speak of the Council in Heaven as a single council, there may have been a number of council meetings where the gospel was taught, where prophets and others were foreordained, and where other assignments were made to individuals. President Joseph Fielding Smith made the following statement about councils in premortal life: "When the time arrived for us to be advanced in the scale of our existence and pass through this mundane probation, councils were held and the spirit children were instructed in matters pertaining to conditions in mortal life, and the reason for such an existence" (*Doctrines of Salvation*, 1:57).

We know that at one point in the proceedings, Heavenly Father's plan for our eternal progress and joy was announced to His spirit sons and daughters. As participants, we had the privilege of accepting or rejecting the plan as it was proposed, and so I'm sure we paid careful attention to discussions of the Creation of the world, the Fall of Adam and Eve, the Atonement, the Resurrection, and the Final Judgment (see "Council in Heaven," in Ludlow, *Encyclopedia of Mormonism,* 1:328-29). We "shouted for joy" (Job 38:7) at the prospect of mortality and its promise and potential, although we may have felt some concern about the possibility of failure.

We know that Satan sought to amend the plan in order to exalt himself above God (see Moses 4:1; Isaiah 14:12-14). Because the issue of agency was crucial to our Father's plan (see D&C 29:35; Moses 4:1, 3) and because He chose His Beloved Son who had volunteered to be the Redeemer (Moses 4:2), Lucifer rebelled and became Satan and persuaded a third of the hosts of heaven to follow him. There followed what is referred to as a War in Heaven, resulting in these rebellious spirits being cast out (Moses 4:3-4; Abraham 3:28).

Of course, we don't know everything that happened during that premortal council. But based on what we do know, Heavenly Father's administration of the Grand Council profoundly illustrates several key principles in decision making through councils.

AN EFFECTIVE LEADER HAS A SENSE OF VISION

First, as council leader, God came to the council with a plan. While it is true that our earthly councils can be effectively used to actually formulate plans of action, it is also true that the leader must come to the council with, at the very least, a sense of vision. That vision doesn't necessarily have to include every detail of *what we want to do.* But if the council is going to arrive at any meaningful decisions, the leader needs to know *where we want to go* and *what we want to have happen.* Without that leadership and sense of vision, how will the council ever know when an appropriate decision has been made?

When a leader in the Church inspires council members with vision, he helps them focus on their real mission so that they are ministering to people rather than merely administering programs. At the same time, this focus builds a strong team spirit that improves working relationships among all members of the council.

Vision makes all the difference in the world. Why was Nephi's reaction to his father's willingness to follow the Lord's direction and lead his family into the wilderness so different from that of his elder brothers, Laman and Lemuel? Could it be because Nephi went to the Lord privately and asked for his own witness or vision of the Lord's directive to his father? "And it came to pass that I, Nephi, being exceedingly young, nevertheless being large in stature, and also having great desires to know of the mysteries of God, wherefore, I did cry unto the Lord; and behold he did visit me, and did soften my heart that I did believe all the words which had been spoken by my father; wherefore, I did not rebel against him like unto my brothers" (1 Nephi 2:16). Nephi sought his own vision, and the result was that his heart was softened. He had a clearer view of where his family was headed, and he was able to commit to follow the Lord. As Solomon explained, "Where there is no vision, the people perish" (Proverbs 29:18).

Almost universally, people become motivated when they feel a sense of purpose and feel as if they are part of a greater cause. It is the privilege and responsibility of leaders to provide those whom they lead with a clear and overpowering sense of vision.

AN EFFECTIVE LEADER ENCOURAGES FREE EXPRESSION

Second, the Grand Council allowed different plans to be heard. What Satan proposed to those assembled was far different from Heavenly Father's plan. Obviously Satan's arguments were persuasive, because many of our spirit brothers and sisters chose to follow him. Similarly, our councils should always allow time for discussion and consideration of differing points of view. We may not always agree with everything others say, but we will all grow from having the opportunity to express ourselves and to consider opinions or approaches to a problem that may vary greatly from our own.

Such experiences, however, underscore the need for leaders to be prepared—mentally, emotionally, and spiritually—and to have carefully and prayerfully considered the matter at hand so that they can establish the vision mentioned previously. A significant aspect of the mantle of leadership, particularly as it applies to the presiding authority, is the privilege and responsibility of marking the course for the larger group, of clearly indicating where the council needs to go.

AN EFFECTIVE LEADER RESPECTS THE GIFT OF AGENCY

Another important principle we observe in the Grand Council in Heaven is that all of the council members had the precious gift of agency. This was not an exercise in compulsion, nor was it a study in domination—even though a case could certainly be made that if ever there was a council that was led by a leader worthy to wield absolute authority, this was the one. Rather, it was an exercise in agency. By making this most significant of all eternal decisions through council, Heavenly Father provided the ultimate illustration of how free and open expression coupled with visionary leadership generally encourages good decision making. Although freedom always brings with it certain risks, challenges, and responsibilities, it also brings real power to those who choose to exercise it wisely. And it gives to all who are so endowed a degree of ownership for council decisions, which experience has shown to be a key element in the successfully functioning council. None could complain that they did not understand or have the opportunity to participate.

If the Grand Council provides us with an excellent illustration of gospel governance through large councils (such as ward councils and stake high councils), another premortal council teaches important lessons about working with smaller, more intimate groups (such as presidencies and bishoprics). In the Pearl of Great Price we learn that a council of Gods, operating under the direction of God our Heavenly Father, worked together to physically create the world on which we live: "And then the Lord said: Let us go down. And they went down at the beginning, and they, that is the Gods, organized and formed the heavens and the earth" (Abraham 4:1).

Throughout the entire creative period this council worked closely together, receiving specific instructions from God, carefully carrying out these instructions, and then returning and reporting their progress while awaiting further instructions. When the time came to create man, Abraham tells us, "the Gods took counsel among themselves" about how this was to be done. They determined to "go down and form man in our image, after our likeness; and we will give them dominion over the fish of the sea, and over the fowl of the air, and over the cattle, and over all the earth, and over every creeping thing that creepeth upon the earth" (Abraham 4:26).

We'll reserve most of our discussion about presidencies, bishoprics, and other small councils for chapter 6. But we need to consider in this chapter several principles illustrated by the Creation council, because these principles apply to Church leaders and councils at all levels.

AN EFFECTIVE LEADER GIVES CLEAR, PRECISE INSTRUCTIONS

The Creation story offers important lessons for those who serve in bishoprics and other councils of presidency. For presiding officers such as presidents and bishops, the Creation outlines three great leadership keys for accomplishment through council. First, notice how Heavenly Father issued clear, precise instructions. He sent His chosen representatives out with clearly defined expectations and then let them decide how best to accomplish the details.

One stake president I know learned the hard way about the importance of issuing such instructions. During a stake presidency meeting he mentioned to his second counselor that he thought it was about time to reorganize the stake Primary presidency. The counselor agreed and awaited further discussion or instruction. When none was forthcoming, the counselor assumed that meant the president wanted him to proceed. At the next stake presidency meeting, the counselor reported that a new stake Primary president had been called and was currently considering counselor options.

The stake president was stunned. "I didn't want the Primary president released," he said. "I just felt that it was time to change her counselors and maybe a few board members!"

If he had simply taken the time to communicate clearly with his counselor, this good stake president could have avoided an extraordinarily uncomfortable situation. Further, the second counselor should have clarified his assignment with his file leader instead of acting upon an assumption when it came to such an important issue. At least in that matter, this presidency's pattern of communication left something to be desired.

AN EFFECTIVE LEADER WORKS STEP BY STEP

The second leadership lesson of the Creation for presidents, bishops, group leaders, and parents has to do with the breadth and the pace of the instructions God issued. He did not say to His council members, "Go out and create a world." Although He had the full vision of what He wanted to have happen, He took His council through the process one step at a time, providing plenty of opportunity for reporting, counsel, and follow-up instruction along the way.

One bishop I know understood immediately upon his calling that his biggest challenge was going to be the ward Aaronic Priesthood program. Not only was that his most pressing responsibility according to divine mandate, but it was an especially vexing concern in his ward, where the Aaronic Priesthood was facing some unusual challenges. As he sat with his counselors for their first bishopric meeting, considerable anguish was expressed over the situation.

"I'm afraid we've already lost a few of these boys," one counselor observed.

"And those who are coming to church will probably resent it if we try to get them to do anything more than what they have been doing on activity night," the other counselor added.

The bishop had been prayerfully considering this most important responsibility ever since his new calling had been extended, and he had a pretty clear vision of what needed to be done. But he also understood that it couldn't happen all at once. Instead, the new bishopric moved through the process one step at a time.

"Who's the strongest priesthood leader in the ward at working with young men?" the bishop asked.

Both counselors immediately named a man who was serving in a stake calling at the time. The bishop considered the man thoughtfully for a few moments. Yes, it felt right.

"Don't you think he would be a great deacons quorum adviser?" the bishop asked.

"Of course," his first counselor said. "He'd be great at anything you called him to. But assuming you can get him from the stake, don't you think it would be better to make him Young Men president so he could control the entire program?"

"Brethren," the bishop said, "*we* are the Aaronic Priesthood presidency of this ward. If anyone is going to 'control' the program, it's going to be us. But if we are going to rebuild the program, we need to do it from the ground up. And it seems to me that means starting out with the strongest deacons quorum we can possibly create."

The counselors felt the wisdom of what their bishop was saying. The stake president agreed to release the brother to serve in the ward, and before too long the ward had an excellent deacons quorum. Its success eventually carried over to the teachers and priests quorums. By the time the bishop was released, every Aaronic Priesthood holder was ready to serve a mission, and the ward had one of the finest Aaronic Priesthood programs in the stake, if not in the entire Church. This happened in part because the bishop understood the process of working through council one step at a time. It's interesting to note that the entire stake Aaronic Priesthood program improved because of the example of this outstanding deacons quorum.

AN EFFECTIVE LEADER DELEGATES

The third lesson that presidents, bishops, group leaders, and parents can learn from the Creation council is that Heavenly Father didn't do all of the work Himself—even though He certainly could have. As God, He had all of the authority and power He needed to create the world, and He clearly was the one who had the full vision of the project. Still He chose to delegate responsibilities, always asking for a follow-up report to make sure that the work had been done correctly.

Why would He do such a thing, especially when it probably would have been faster and more efficient for Him to simply do it Himself? In my view, one reason He did it was to establish a pattern for us to follow. By delegating so important a work as the creation of the earth, He left us precious little room to justify our own feelings of self-importance when we are unwilling to delegate in our Church callings and offices.

I heard recently about a new ward Relief Society president who decided she needed to visit sisters in the ward personally on their birthdays. Then she decided she should take a birthday greeting, so she wrote a quick note to each sister to take with her when she visited. Then she decided the note should be attached to a fresh loaf of homemade bread, which she would make herself. Then she decided that the bread and the note should be wrapped in a clever linen cloth, which she would quickly sew herself. Then she decided that the bundle needed a jar of her homemade preserves to go along with it.

After making her birthday deliveries for a few months, this sister dragged herself into the bishop's office and asked to be released.

"It's too much work," she said. "I just can't do it."

It didn't take long for the bishop to cut through to the core of the problem. "The birthday greeting is a fine idea," he said, "but maybe you need a little help." The bishop explained that there were certain tasks she alone should handle; all others could be delegated. Counseling together, they came up with a way to give several sisters a chance to participate in a toned-down version of the birthday project, opening opportunities of fellowship and service to some women who were in desperate need of such involvement. Through delegation, the president's vision was accomplished without completely draining her of time and energy.

Presidents and bishops should give their highest priority and attention to matters that they alone have the authority to handle, leaving for others—counselors and council members—those tasks that can reasonably be accomplished by someone else. Any leader who becomes bogged down in an endless array of details runs the risk of undermining the effectiveness of his or her own ministry.

There is another reason to delegate, and that is to empower and prepare leaders for future service. One of the most important evidences of effective leadership is the number of well-prepared brothers and sisters who are in place to carry on the work.

The biblical patriarch Jethro gave wise counsel to his son-in-law, Moses, when the elder man visited his daughter's family and saw the constant demands being made by the people upon their prophet. "The thing that thou doest is not good," Jethro said. "Thou wilt surely wear away, both thou, and this people that is with thee: for this thing is too heavy for thee; thou art not able to perform it thyself alone" (Exodus 18:17–18).

Jethro went on to gently teach his son-in-law how to delegate a portion of his responsibilities to others. Not only would such delegation make things easier for Moses, Jethro said, but it would also be a blessing for those who served with him, for "they shall bear the burden with thee" (Exodus 18:22). When you personally shoulder a burden, it becomes more real, more fervent. It is hard to care about issues for which you have no responsibility or which don't touch your life in a meaningful way. And so Jethro's counsel to Moses is excellent advice for today's leaders, too.

AN EFFECTIVE LEADER SETS AN EXAMPLE OF HARD WORK

There are also lessons in the Creation council for those who serve as counselors—lessons on the importance of listening, of carefully following instructions, and of "returning and reporting." But perhaps the most basic principle illustrated by those who carried out Heavenly Father's instructions during the Creation was the principle of "Let us go and do."

When Jehovah was instructed by God to perform certain creative tasks, He did not respond by saying, "Let us see" or "Let us try" or "Let us look for time in our busy schedule." Rather, He simply and powerfully said, "Let us go . . ." (Abraham 4:1). His attitude indicated that He was anxious to *do* His Father's will, not to sit around and talk about it. "I can of mine own self do nothing," the Savior said, " . . . because I seek not mine own will, but the will of the Father which hath sent me" (John 5:30).

The Savior typified that attitude throughout His mortal life. Even as a child He understood the importance of "going" and "doing." When He was missing from the family entourage during a trip from Jerusalem to Nazareth, His parents finally found

Him at the temple, "sitting in the midst of the doctors, both hearing them, and asking them questions.

"And all that heard him were astonished at his understanding and answers.

"And when they saw him, they were amazed: and his mother said unto him, Son, why hast thou thus dealt with us? behold, thy father and I have sought thee sorrowing.

"And he said unto them, How is it that ye sought me? wist ye not that I must be about my Father's business?" (Luke 2:46–49).

Throughout His ministry Jesus taught His followers the importance of *doing*. At the conclusion of the parable of the good Samaritan, in which the value of *doing* was emphasized over pious beliefs and promises, the Savior asked His listener, "Which now of these three, thinkest thou, was neighbour unto him that fell among the thieves?

"And he said, He that shewed mercy on him. Then said Jesus unto him, *Go*, and *do* thou likewise" (Luke 10:36–37; emphasis added).

On another occasion, He reminded His followers that "not every one that saith unto me, Lord, Lord, shall enter into the kingdom of heaven; but he that *doeth* the will of my Father which is in heaven" (Matthew 7:21; emphasis added). And even as He contemplated the painful end of His sojourn in mortality, He underscored His message of eternal commitment to God's will with this humble statement of obedience: "Father, if thou be willing, remove this cup from me: nevertheless not my will, but thine, be done" (Luke 22:42).

Our latter-day prophets are well known for such phrases as "Let's get going," "Do it," "Do it now." I have heard President Gordon B. Hinckley say that the only way he knows to get things done is to first get on his knees and pray, and then to get on his feet and go do the work. That driving desire to "go" and "do" the Lord's will has been the hallmark of our prophet-presidents all of their lives.

Of course, "going and doing" isn't always easy or comfortable. Occasionally it requires some sacrifice on our part—of time, energy, or personal will. But it is almost always worth whatever effort we make, especially if it has to do with following the instructions of inspired council leaders in seeking to bring souls to Christ.

AN EFFECTIVE LEADER TEACHES BY PRECEPT AND EXAMPLE

That Jesus is committed to the council concept cannot be questioned. Twice in ancient times He personally organized His Church on the earth, and both times He established it with governing councils. In both the Holy Land of the New Testament and the promised land of the Book of Mormon, He spent considerable time teaching and instructing and training His councils and council leaders, and then He sent them forth to share what they had learned with others. Although the circumstances surrounding the two experiences were different, they both share at least two key similarities that illustrate the Savior's exemplary administration of councils.

First, He taught His ancient councils carefully—by precept and by example. He instructed them how to pray, and then He prayed with them and for them. He taught them how to conduct the sacred sacrament of the Lord's Supper, and then He blessed bread and wine and gave it to them. He told them how to use their priesthood authority to bless the lives of others, and then He used His priesthood authority to work miracles among them.

Near the end of His mortal ministry, Jesus celebrated the Feast of the Passover with His beloved disciples. Although He was facing the final, climactic moments of His life, with their attendant pain and suffering, His attention was focused on those who followed Him. After the feast was over,

> he riseth from supper, and laid aside his garments; and took a towel, and girded himself.
>
> After that he poureth water into a basin, and began to wash the disciples' feet, and to wipe them with the towel wherewith he was girded.
>
> Then cometh he to Simon Peter: and Peter saith unto him, Lord, dost thou wash my feet?
>
> Jesus answered and said unto him, What I do thou knowest not now; but thou shalt know hereafter.
>
> Peter saith unto him, Thou shalt never wash my feet. Jesus answered him, If I wash thee not, thou hast no part with me.
>
> Simon Peter saith unto him, Lord, not my feet only, but also my hands and my head. . . .
>
> So after he had washed their feet, and had taken his garments, and was set down again, he said unto them, Know ye what I have done to you?
>
> Ye call me Master and Lord: and ye say well; for so I am.
>
> If I then, your Lord and Master, have washed your feet; ye also ought to wash one another's feet.
>
> For I have given you an example, that ye should do as I have done to you.
>
> Verily, verily, I say unto you, The servant is not greater than his lord; neither he that is sent greater than he that sent him.
>
> If ye know these things, happy are ye if ye do them. (John 13:4–9, 12–17)

Oh, that all council leaders could understand the value of

service one to another as taught in this powerful example of the Savior!

AN EFFECTIVE LEADER SERVES WITH LOVE

Second, He loved those with whom He served in council. "As the Father hath loved me, so have I loved you," He told His Apostles (John 15:9). Then He added, "This is my commandment, That ye love one another, as I have loved you" (John 15:12).

"A new commandment I give unto you, That ye love one another; as I have loved you, that ye also love one another. By this shall all men know that ye are my disciples, if ye have love one to another" (John 13:34-35).

How critical it is that all who serve together in God's kingdom do so from a foundation of love: love for the Lord, love for the work, and love for each other. No matter how intense our effort or how carefully we follow the handbooks and guidelines, if we don't truly love each other we can't possibly hope to convey the full power of the gospel of love. And I can't help but believe that members are more likely to seek counsel from leaders from whom they feel sincere love emanating. Miracles seem to follow after Church leaders who are motivated by a keen feeling of loving devotion to those over whom they preside.

As I travel throughout the Church, I've noticed that stake congregations tend to reflect the attitudes and relationships of their leaders. Whenever I sense a spirit of loving brotherhood and cooperation among members of the stake presidency, that same spirit inevitably seems to permeate every stake meeting I attend. Unfortunately, the opposite is also true.

"Beloved," wrote the Apostle John, "let us love one another: for love is of God; and every one that loveth is born of God, and knoweth God.

"He that loveth not knoweth not God; for God is love.

"In this was manifested the love of God toward us, because

that God sent his only begotten Son into the world, that we might live through him.

"Herein is love, not that we loved God, but that he loved us, and sent his Son to be the propitiation for our sins.

"Beloved, if God so loved us, we ought also to love one another" (1 John 4:7–11).

A ward with which I'm familiar experienced a dramatic increase in attendance by less-active members when a new bishop used ten minutes of each ward council meeting to discuss ways council members could reach out to those in need—spiritually and temporally. Under the direction of this easy-going, compassionate bishop, fellowshipping assignments were made, pairing people with common interests. During the course of a three-year period, as council members showed love and consideration for those with whom they labored, nearly a dozen families were reactivated.

MAKING A DIFFERENCE

And so, from the very beginning, "God so loved the world, that he gave his only begotten Son, that whosoever believeth in him should not perish, but have everlasting life" (John 3:16). From those premortal councils came our opportunity to come to earth to work out our own salvation through the grace and love of the Lord Jesus Christ.

With the love of Christ reflecting from all Church councils and radiating throughout an entire quorum, auxiliary, ward, or stake, a significant difference can be made in our lives and in the lives of our family members as well as all of our Heavenly Father's children. And making a difference in people's lives is, after all, the great mission of Church councils, which had their beginning in the heavenly councils we saw and experienced in our premortal lives.

CHAPTER 2

GENERAL COUNCILS IN THE CHURCH

Sometime late in June 1829, an important transition took place in the history of the Restoration of the gospel of Jesus Christ. With the translation of the Book of Mormon completed, Joseph Smith invited his family to join him at the home of Peter Whitmer in Fayette, New York, where they would be allowed for the first time to read the work that had been a consuming focus for many months.

As soon as they arrived in Fayette, a small group that included Joseph, his parents, Martin Harris, Oliver Cowdery, and David Whitmer began reading the manuscript. "We rejoiced exceedingly," wrote Joseph's mother, Lucy Mack Smith, of the occasion. "It then appeared to those of us who did not realize the magnitude of the work, as if the greatest difficulty was then surmounted" (Smith, *History of Joseph Smith by His Mother,* 151).

Although Joseph was just beginning the long and arduous process of the Restoration, he was ready for some help. Though there were many who believed in him and supported his work, sometimes at great personal risk and expense, there were none called to share the burden of the significant stewardship that had been placed upon him. For the previous nine years, he had stood mostly alone in his work and testimony.

And so it must have been with joyful anticipation that Joseph approached Martin during the group's morning devotional services the day after his arrival in Fayette and said, "Martin Harris, you have got to humble yourself before God this day, that you may obtain a forgiveness of your sins. If you do, it is the will of God that you should look upon the plates, in company with Oliver Cowdery and David Whitmer."

Lucy Mack Smith, who was present that morning, said those words were spoken "with a solemnity that thrills through my veins to this day, when it occurs to my recollection" (ibid., 152).

According to revelation, the Lord commanded Joseph to extend the call to Martin Harris, Oliver Cowdery, and David Whitmer to serve as special witnesses of the Book of Mormon

that my servant Joseph Smith, Jun., may not be destroyed, that I may bring about my righteous purposes unto the children of men in this work.

And ye shall testify that you have seen them, even as my servant Joseph Smith, Jun., has seen them; for it is by my power that he has seen them, and it is because he had faith.

And he has translated the book, even that part which I have commanded him, and as your Lord and your God liveth it is true.

Wherefore, you have received the same power, and the same faith, and the same gift like unto him;

And if you do these last commandments of mine, which I have given you, the gates of hell shall not prevail against you; for my grace is sufficient for you, and you shall be lifted up at the last day.

And I, Jesus Christ, your Lord and your God, have

spoken it unto you, that I might bring about my righteous purposes unto the children of men. Amen. (D&C 17:4-9)

Soon after the call to witness was extended, the four men retired to a nearby grove of trees to receive the promised revelation. Later that afternoon they returned to the Whitmer home, where Joseph exclaimed, "Father, mother, you do not know how happy I am: the Lord has now caused the plates to be shown to three more besides myself. They have seen an angel, who has testified to them, and they will have to bear witness to the truth of what I have said, for now they know for themselves, that I do not go about to deceive the people, and I feel as if I was relieved of a burden which was almost too heavy for me to bear, and it rejoices my soul, that I am not any longer to be entirely alone in the world" (Smith, *History of Joseph Smith by His Mother,* 152). Less than a year later, The Church of Jesus Christ of Latter-day Saints was officially organized with Joseph Smith as "the first elder of this church" and Oliver Cowdery as "the second elder of this church" (D&C 20:2, 3). At the same time, the Lord revealed His instructions to the Apostles, elders, priests, teachers, deacons, and members of the Church, outlining specific duties and responsibilities for each as they accepted their share of stewardship within Joseph's ministry. Eventually the Church was organized into quorums and councils, with various presidencies appointed "to administer in spiritual things" (D&C 107:8).

According to revelation, "the decisions of these quorums . . . are to be made in all righteousness, in holiness, and lowliness of heart, meekness and long suffering, and in faith, and virtue, and knowledge, temperance, patience, godliness, brotherly kindness and charity; because the promise is, if these things abound in them they shall not be unfruitful in the knowledge of the Lord" (D&C 107:30-31).

"Wherefore," the Lord continued, "now let every man learn his duty, and to act in the office in which he is appointed, in all diligence. He that is slothful shall not be counted worthy to stand, and he that learns not his duty and shows himself not approved shall not be counted worthy to stand" (D&C 107:99–100).

Having experienced the spiritual loneliness of his early ministry and having subsequently been tutored of the Lord, Joseph Smith had profound appreciation for the important work of councils in the Church of Jesus Christ. Soon after the first high council was organized, the Prophet

> laid [his] hands upon the twelve Councilors, and commanded a blessing to rest upon them, that they might have wisdom and power to counsel in righteousness, upon all subjects that might be laid before them. I also prayed that they might be delivered from those evils to which they were most exposed, and that their lives might be prolonged on the earth. . . .
>
> I then gave the assistant Presidents a solemn charge to do their duty in righteousness, and in the fear of God; I also charged the twelve Councilors in a similar manner, all in the name of Jesus Christ.
>
> We all raised our hands to heaven in token of the everlasting covenant, and the Lord blessed us with His Spirit. I then declared the council organized according to the ancient order, and also according to the mind of the Lord. (*History of the Church*, 2:32–33)

As committed as they were to God's service, however, Joseph Smith's followers occasionally struggled with the council concept. The Prophet recorded:

> At a council of the High Priests and Elders . . . at my house in Kirtland, on the evening of the 12th of

February [1834], I remarked that I should endeavor to set before the council the dignity of the office which had been conferred on me by the ministering of the angel of God, by His own voice, and by the voice of this Church; that I had never set before any council in all the order in which it ought to be conducted, which, perhaps, has deprived the councils of some or many blessings.

And I continued and said, no man is capable of judging a matter, in council, unless his own heart is pure; and that we are frequently so filled with prejudice, or have a beam in our own eye, that we are not capable of passing right decisions.

But to return to the subject of order; in ancient days councils were conducted with such strict propriety, that no one was allowed to whisper, be weary, leave the room, or get uneasy in the least, until the voice of the Lord, by revelation, or the voice of the council by the Spirit, was obtained, which has not been observed in this Church to the present time. It was understood in ancient days, that if one man could stay in council, another could; and if the president could spend his time, the members could also; but in our councils, generally, one will be uneasy, another asleep; one praying, another not; one's mind on the business of the council, and another thinking on something else.

Our acts are recorded, and at a future day they will be laid before us, and if we should fail to judge right and injure our fellow-beings, they may there, perhaps, condemn us; there they are of great consequence, and to me the consequence appears to be of force, beyond anything which I am able to express. Ask yourselves, brethren, how much you have exercised yourselves in prayer since you heard of this council; and if you are now prepared to sit in council upon the soul of your brother. (*History of the Church,* 2:25-26)

One year later, almost to the day, the Lord revealed additional information to Joseph Smith about how council governance could help relieve some of the pressure he was feeling as leader of the Church:

On the 8th day of February, in the year of our Lord 1835, the Prophet Joseph Smith called Elders Brigham and Joseph Young to the chamber of his residence, in Kirtland, Ohio, it being on the Sabbath day. After they were seated and he had made some preliminaries, he proceeded to relate a vision to these brethren, of the state and condition of those men who died in Zion's Camp, in Missouri. He said, "Brethren, I have seen those men who died of the cholera in our camp; and the Lord knows, if I get a mansion as bright as theirs, I ask no more." At this revelation he wept, and for some time could not speak. When he had relieved himself of his feelings, in describing the vision, he resumed the conversation, and addressed himself to Brother Brigham Young. He said to him, "I wish you to notify all the brethren living in the branches, within a reasonable distance from this place, to meet at a general conference on Saturday next. I shall then and there appoint twelve Special Witnesses, to open the door of the Gospel to foreign nations, and you," said he (speaking to Brother Brigham), "will be one of them." He then proceeded to enlarge upon the duties of their calling. The interest that was taken on the occasion of this announcement, produced in the minds of the two Elders present a great sensation and many reflections; having previously notified Brother Brigham Young that he would be one of the Witnesses, but said nothing to

Joseph, until he had exhausted much of his feelings in regard to the Twelve, which took up some little time. He then turned to Elder Joseph Young with quite an earnestness, as though the vision of his mind was extended still further, and addressing him, said, "Brother Joseph, the Lord has made you President of the Seventies." They had heard of Moses and seventy Elders of Israel, and of Jesus appointing "other Seventies," but had never heard of Twelve Apostles and of Seventies being called in this Church before. It was a strange saying, "The Lord has made you President of the Seventies," as though it had already taken place, and it caused these brethren to marvel. The Prophet did not say that any others would be called to be the bearers of this message abroad, but the inference might be clearly drawn, that this was his meaning, from the language he used at the time. Agreeable to his request to Elder Brigham Young, the branches were all notified, and a meeting of the brethren in general conference was held in Kirtland, in the new school house under the printing office, on the following Saturday, February 14th, when the Twelve were appointed and ordained, and the conference adjourned for two weeks. (Joseph Young, Sr., "History of the Organization of the Seventies" [1878], 1–2; quoted in *History of the Church*, 2:181)

General Church Councils

Through the years, the forms and formats of Church governance and administration have been adjusted to meet changing needs and times. But they have always been characterized by reliance upon councils for ongoing solidarity and strength. President Stephen L Richards said in 1953:

I don't know that it is possible for any organization to succeed in the Church . . . without adopting the genius of our Church government. What is that? As I conceive it, the genius of our Church government is government through *councils.* The Council of the Presidency, the Council of the Twelve, the Council of the Stake Presidency, or quorum, if you choose to use that word, the Council of the Bishopric, and the quorum [or] Council of the Quorum Presidency. I have had enough experience to know the value of councils. Hardly a day passes but that I see the wisdom, God's wisdom, in creating councils . . . to govern his Kingdom. In the spirit under which we labor, men can get together with seemingly divergent views and far different backgrounds, and under the operation of that spirit, by counseling together, they can arrive at an accord, and that accord . . . represents the wisdom of the council, acting under the Spirit. (In Conference Report, Oct. 1953, 86; emphasis in original)

As it was in Joseph Smith's day, the presiding council of The Church of Jesus Christ of Latter-day Saints today is the First Presidency. It consists of the President of the Church and his two Counselors. According to scriptural mandate, "the keys of the kingdom . . . belong always unto the Presidency of the High Priesthood" (D&C 81:2). The members of this council are sustained by the entire body of the Church as "prophets, seers, and revelators," those to whom it is given "to receive the oracles for the whole church" (D&C 124:126), and they "have a right to officiate in all the offices in the church" (D&C 107:9).

During my term of service in the Quorum of the Twelve Apostles, I have had the privilege of watching the First Presidency function in a wide variety of situations and circumstances. While I have always been impressed by the strengths and abilities of the individual men who compose the Presidency, I have been inspired almost to the point of being overwhelmed by the powerful way they work as an exemplary council and continue to do so even when not all members of the council are fully able to function.

Next in Church authority to the First Presidency is the Quorum of the Twelve Apostles, the council to which I belong. According to scripture, the Apostles are called as "especial witnesses" of the name of Christ (D&C 27:12) with the specific mission "to declare my gospel, both unto Gentile and unto Jew" (D&C 18:26). As a council "they form a quorum, equal in authority and power" to the First Presidency (D&C 107:24). As President Joseph Fielding Smith explained, this means that the Twelve "have power to assume control of the affairs of the Church when the Presidency is dissolved by the death of the President" (*Doctrines of Salvation,* 1:255). Indeed, when the President of the Church dies, the First Presidency is immediately suspended, the President's Counselors return to their respective places in the Quorum of the Twelve Apostles, and the Quorum presides over the Church until a new President is appointed. In my twelve years of service in the Quorum of the Twelve, I have participated in this process three times, witnessing the formation of a new First Presidency under each of three modern-day prophets: Presidents Ezra Taft Benson, Howard W. Hunter, and Gordon B. Hinckley. Except for brief interim periods after the death of a President of the Church, the Quorum of the Twelve functions in its scriptural stewardship to "teach, expound, exhort, baptize, and watch over the church" (D&C 20:42).

The development of "The Family: A Proclamation to the World" is a good example of how the council process works. During the course of our regular meetings, the concept of the proclamation was agreed to by the First Presidency and the Quorum of the Twelve Apostles because of the great need that exists in the Church as well as in the entire world to understand the divinely ordained role of the home and family. The Quorum of the Twelve Apostles is composed of a diverse group of men who possess extraordinary spiritual capabilities, and we drew upon all of that sensitivity in drafting the document. It required numerous revisions and adjustments, which were attended to in our council meetings, before the First Presidency approved it to be sent forth to the whole world. Every member of the Church should read and understand this most important proclamation.

We recognize that it is no small thing for the world to receive such a proclamation and warning from the First Presidency and the Quorum of the Twelve Apostles. Our task was accomplished by drawing upon the diversity of backgrounds, abilities, and spiritual gifts of the members of the Quorum and by utilizing the Lord's inspired program of counseling with our councils.

Speaking of both the First Presidency and the Quorum of the Twelve, the Lord said that "the decisions of these quorums, or either of them, are to be made in all righteousness, in holiness, and lowliness of heart, meekness and long suffering, and in faith, and virtue, and knowledge, temperance, patience, godliness, brotherly kindness and charity; because the promise is, if these things abound in them they shall not be unfruitful in the knowledge of the Lord" (D&C 107:30–31).

That is a promise that is vitally important to all who serve in these important Church councils.

Elder Rulon G. Craven, a former member of the Second Quorum of the Seventy, once described the decision-making process that is followed in meetings of the Quorum of the Twelve Apostles:

It has been my privilege as Executive Secretary to the Quorum of the Twelve to sit in some of the leading councils of the Church and witness the communication processes that take place in conducting the business of the Church. From these experiences, I have witnessed that the business of the Church is carried out under the influence of the Spirit. I know that the righteousness of the individuals who sit in those councils contributes much to the inspiration and the effectiveness of the council meetings.

It has been interesting for me to watch the Brethren work from an agenda that contains many items, and see them handle each item efficiently and effectively. I have noticed that each of the Brethren is not so much concerned with expressing his own point of view as he is with listening to the point of view of others and striving to create a proper climate in the Council meetings. They are sensitive to one another's thoughts and rarely interrupt one another during their conversations. During discussion they do not push their own ideas but try to determine from the discussion what would be best for the kingdom.

Let me share with you a typical experience in a meeting of the Quorum of the Twelve. They always work from an agenda. The agenda is distributed to each member of the Twelve the night before the meeting so that they have an opportunity to read, ponder, and consider each item in preparation for the meeting. When they meet together they usually express love and concern for one another. After an opening prayer, in which a request is made for the Spirit to be in the meeting, the President of the Twelve addresses each item on the agenda one by one. He may make some short preparatory comments that he feels necessary concerning the item, and then he presents the item or asks one of the Twelve to present the item for discussion.

The Brethren express their thoughts and feelings.

They are men of strong character, men from different backgrounds—they are certainly not "yes" men. They speak as they are moved by the Spirit. They strive to feel the manifestations of the Spirit concerning the item being discussed, which may necessitate a change in their own feelings and thoughts in order to be in harmony with the entire Council. When the President of the Twelve senses a unity taking place concerning the item on the agenda, he may ask for a recommendation, or one of the Twelve may present a recommendation to the Twelve. The recommendation remarkably summarizes the feelings of the total Council. The President will then state, "We have before us a recommendation. Is there any further discussion?" Each member of the Twelve will have an opportunity again to express himself. They don't repeat what has already been said; rather, there is an unusual economy of expression in order to ascertain the total views of the Council. After all who have a desire to speak have done so, the recommendation may be modified. The recommendation is then presented in the form of a motion by a member of the Twelve, and is seconded by another. The President of the Twelve then asks for the vote of the Quorum; thus, the Twelve make decisions in harmony, unity, and faith, with the combined judgment of each member and in harmony with the Spirit. (*Called to the Work*, 111-13)

As President Gordon B. Hinckley has explained, it is through the council meetings of the First Presidency and the Quorum of the Twelve Apostles, held each week in the Salt Lake Temple, that the Church is governed by revelation:

Any major questions of policy, procedures, programs, or doctrine are considered deliberately and prayerfully by the First Presidency and the Twelve together. These two quorums, the Quorum of the First Presidency and the Quorum of the Twelve, meeting together, with every man having total freedom to express himself, consider every major question.

And now I quote . . . from the word of the Lord: "And every decision made by either of these quorums must be by the unanimous voice of the same; that is, every member in each quorum must be agreed to its decisions, in order to make their decisions of the same power or validity one with the other" (D&C 107:27).

No decision emanates from the deliberations of the First Presidency and the Twelve without total unanimity among all concerned. At the outset in considering matters, there may be differences of opinion. These are to be expected. These men come from different backgrounds. They are men who think for themselves. But before a final decision is reached, there comes a unanimity of mind and voice. . . .

I add by way of personal testimony that during the twenty years I served as a member of the Council of the Twelve and during the . . . years that I have served in the First Presidency, there has never been a major action taken where this procedure was not observed. I have seen differences of opinion presented in these deliberations. Out of this very process of men speaking their minds has come a sifting and winnowing of ideas and concepts. But I have never observed serious discord or personal enmity among my Brethren. I have, rather, observed a beautiful and remarkable thing—the coming together, under the directing influence of the Holy Spirit and under the power of revelation, of divergent views until there is total harmony and full agreement. Only then is implementation made. That, I testify, represents the spirit of revelation manifested again and again in directing this the Lord's work. ("God Is at the Helm," 54, 59)

There are other examples of authoritative quorums and councils that function on behalf of the entire Church: the Presidency of the Seventy, the Quorums of the Seventy, the Presiding Bishopric, and the general auxiliary presidencies (Relief Society, Young Women, Young Men, Sunday School, and Primary) and their respective boards. There are also a variety of committees that function as councils under General Authority direction as they administer specific areas of responsibility. Although the specific assignments and respective areas of focus may shift from time to time, the successful application of council concepts is absolutely essential to their effectiveness in the overall gospel plan.

Similar councils operate throughout the world in the various areas, stakes, missions, districts, wards, and branches of the Church. We'll consider these councils in more detail in later chapters. But there is one critical issue that needs to be explored first because it has significant application to many Church councils.

THE ROLE OF WOMEN IN CHURCH COUNCILS

As you consider the numerous councils and committees that exist throughout the Church organization, you will notice that they are priesthood-directed. There is a good reason for that. As President John Taylor once said, the priesthood is "the government of God, whether on the earth or in the heavens, for it is by that power, agency, or principle that all things are governed on the earth and in the heavens, and by that power that all things are upheld and sustained. It governs all things—it directs all things—it sustains all things—and has to do with all things that

God and truth are associated with" (*Millennial Star,* 1 Nov. 1847, 321; quoted in Taylor, *Gospel Kingdom,* 129).

At the same time, it must be remembered by all who hold priesthood authority that "the rights of the priesthood are inseparably connected with the powers of heaven, and that the powers of heaven cannot be controlled nor handled only upon the principles of righteousness" (D&C 121:36).

And what are those "principles of righteousness" through which one can control—or at least draw upon—"the powers of heaven"? The Lord taught Joseph Smith that priesthood power or influence is maintained through such traits as "persuasion . . . long-suffering . . . gentleness . . . meekness . . . love unfeigned . . . kindness, and pure knowledge, which shall greatly enlarge the soul without hypocrisy, and without guile" (D&C 121:41-42). As I consider the traits and characteristics through which God empowers His people, I find them to be consistent with the sensitive attributes that are part of the rich tradition of spirituality, gentleness, meekness, love, and kindness found among many of the women of the Church. And I am aware that there is much of persuasion, long-suffering, and pure knowledge, and little of hypocrisy and guile, among the women who typically serve in the Church councils to which they are assigned, either generally or locally.

In an address to Regional Representatives in 1989, Elder Marvin J. Ashton of the Quorum of the Twelve Apostles said:

> We . . . recognize the significance and virtues of the strong supporting work of the auxiliaries, especially those headed by our women—the Primary, the Young Women, and the Relief Society. As both the quorums and the auxiliaries are strengthened and begin to fulfill their responsibility in accomplishing the mission of the Church, the singular burden currently carried by the bishops in so many areas will be relieved. . . . We are not

unmindful of the women of the Church. The work of our wonderful women is vital. . . . It is extremely important for stake and ward councils and committees to consistently concern themselves with the issues that affect the families, women, youth, and children. These issues should be a regular part of the agenda of these meetings, and our women leaders should take part in the discussions. Our women are companion-leaders to help all of our members receive the benefits of the Church and the watch care, development, and refuge from the world that the Church provides. Please do not overlook the great strength that can and does come from our women. (Address at Regional Representatives' seminar, 31 Mar. 1989, 2)

Consider also this statement from President Gordon B. Hinckley:

What a resource are the women of The Church of Jesus Christ of Latter-day Saints. You love this Church, you accept its doctrine, you honor your place in its organization, you bring luster and strength and beauty to its congregations. How thankful we are to you. How much you are loved, respected, and honored. . . .

You bring a measure of wholeness to us. You have great strength. With dignity and tremendous ability, you carry forward the remarkable programs of the Relief Society, the Young Women, and the Primary. You teach Sunday School. We walk at your side as your companions and your brethren with respect and love, with honor and great admiration. It was the Lord who designated that men in His Church should hold the priesthood. It was He who has given you your capabilities to round out this great and marvelous organization, which is the Church and kingdom of God. I bear testimony before the entire world of your worth, of your grace and goodness, of your remarkable abilities and tremendous contributions. ("Women of the Church," 70)

This wise counsel of the President of the Church conveys the spirit of the role of women as they participate in the stake and ward councils of the Church. Stronger testimonies and deeper commitment are needed, and sister leaders can assist the priesthood in finding solutions and in teaching, strengthening, and preparing mothers, young women, and children to have a greater love for and dedication to the Lord Jesus Christ and His Church.

Therefore, I would urge the priesthood brethren who preside over ward and stake councils to draw upon the great power, insight, and wisdom that women can bring with them to these council meetings. Our sisters can contribute the power of faith, through which "the worlds were framed by the word of God" (Hebrews 11:3). They can bring the power of purity, through which "we may be purified even as [the Lord] is pure" (Moroni 7:48). And they generally possess the power of love, that which the Apostle Paul called charity, the greatest of all godly virtues (see 1 Corinthians 13:13). It is a short-sighted priesthood leader who does not see the value of calling upon the sisters to share the understanding and inspiration they possess.

One general Church auxiliary leader told me about a marvelous experience she had with her bishop when she was serving as a ward Relief Society president. "I had been serving for only a short time when this new bishop was called," she said. "One of the first things he did after he was ordained and set apart to his new calling was to ask me to come to his office to visit with him. He said, 'I want you to know that it is impossible for me to fulfill my calling and to fulfill my responsibilities to the Lord without your input. I want you to let me know the concerns of the sisters, and I want you to know that when you come to ward council, whatever you have to tell us, we will be listening.' That put my respect for my calling on a whole different plane, because I knew that I was needed."

The sisters of the Church *are* needed. Whether you are eighteen or eighty, are married or single, speak English or Portuguese, live on an island or in the mountains, have children or simply love children, have an advanced degree or little formal education, have a husband who is not active or are married to a stake president, you belong here! You and your talents, strengths, and insights are urgently needed in the Church. As Eliza R. Snow, the second general president of the Relief Society, said, "There is no sister so isolated, and her sphere so narrow but what she can do a great deal towards establishing the Kingdom of God upon the earth" (address at a Relief Society meeting, 14 Aug. 1873; quoted in *Woman's Exponent,* 15 Sept. 1873, 62).

Our Father in Heaven loves all of His children equally, perfectly, and infinitely. His love is no different for His daughters than for His sons. Our Savior, the Lord Jesus Christ, also loves men and women equally. His Atonement and His gospel are for all of God's children. During His earthly ministry Jesus served men and women alike: He healed both men and women, and He taught both men and women.

The gospel of Jesus Christ sanctifies both men and women in the same way and by identical principles. For example, the principles of faith and repentance, the ordinance of baptism, and the gift of the Holy Ghost apply equally to all of God's children, regardless of gender. The same is true of temple covenants and blessings; men and women alike must receive all of the ordinances of salvation. Our Father's work and glory is to bring to pass the immortality and eternal life of His children. He loves us all equally, and His greatest gift, the gift of eternal life, is available to all.

Even though men and women are equal before God in their eternal opportunities, they do have different duties in His eternal plan—and yet these differing roles and duties are equally significant. We must understand that God views all of His children with infinite wisdom and perfect fairness. Consequently, He can acknowledge and even encourage our differences while providing equal opportunities for growth and development.

While we lived with Him as His spirit sons and daughters, Heavenly Father assigned different responsibilities in mortality to men and women. To His sons He gave the priesthood and the responsibilities of fatherhood, and to His daughters He gave the responsibilities of motherhood, each with its attendant functions. The Creation of the world, the Atonement of Jesus Christ, and the Restoration of the gospel in the latter days through the Prophet Joseph Smith all have one unifying purpose: to enable all of the spirit children of our Eternal Father to obtain mortal bodies, and then, through the gift of moral agency, to follow the plan of redemption made possible by the Savior's Atonement. God prepared all of this for us that we might return to our heavenly home, clothed in immortality and eternal life, to live with Him as families.

A family can live with Him only after a man and a woman are sealed in marriage for eternity by the power of the holy priesthood. We acknowledge that many in the Church desire this great blessing but have little hope of its fulfillment in this life. Nevertheless, the promise of exaltation remains an attainable goal for each one of us. The prophets have stated clearly that no blessing will be withheld from any of God's sons or daughters if they love Him, have faith in Him, keep His commandments, and endure faithfully to the end.

Most of what men and women must do to qualify for an exalted family life together is based on shared responsibilities and objectives. Many of the requirements are exactly the same for men and women. For example, obedience to the laws of God is required equally of men and women. Requirements for entrance into the temple are the same for both, and all who enter those sacred edifices are eligible to be clothed with power and to find therein a house of learning, a house of glory, a house of God. Men and women should pray in the same way. They both have the same privilege of receiving answers to their prayers and thereby obtaining personal revelation for their own spiritual benefit.

Both men and women are to serve their families and others, but the specific ways in which they do so are sometimes different. For example, God has revealed through His prophets that men are to receive the priesthood, to become fathers, and with gentleness and pure, unfeigned love to lead and nurture their families in righteousness, taking for their pattern the way the Savior leads the Church. Men have also been given the primary responsibility for providing for the temporal and physical needs of the family. Women have the ability to bring children into the world and have been given the primary role and opportunity to lead, nurture, and teach their little ones in a loving, safe, and spiritual environment. In this divinely sanctioned partnership, husbands and wives work together, each bringing his or her unique contribution to the family. Such a couple provide the children born to their union a home where they can be fully nurtured by both a mother and a father. By appointing different accountabilities to men and women, Heavenly Father provides the greatest opportunity for growth, service, and progress.

Why this pattern is the approved pattern is not entirely clear. The Lord has chosen to reveal only His will on the matter, not His reasoning. Indeed, the reasons are unimportant as far as we are concerned, because the issue is not open to debate. Consensus and public opinion are irrelevant to a discussion of the doctrine of God, because it is mandated through revelation, not legislation or negotiation. For us, the only thing that matters is whether or not we choose to accept the doctrine of the priesthood and abide by its precepts. It is an issue of faith—nothing more, nothing less.

Of course, sometimes our faith is tested. It is easy to understand why many sisters are frustrated when they sit in council with priesthood leaders and are not invited to make substantive contributions to the council. They have much to offer in finding real solutions to the problems facing priesthood leaders. Perhaps the Lord had in mind the arrogant priesthood leader who would ignore or dismiss the wisdom of any council member when He gave this warning to the Prophet Joseph Smith: "When we undertake to cover our sins, or to gratify our pride, our vain ambition, or to exercise control or dominion or compulsion upon the souls of the children of men, in any degree of unrighteousness, behold, the heavens withdraw themselves; the Spirit of the Lord is grieved; and when it is withdrawn, Amen to the priesthood or the authority of that man" (D&C 121:37).

In other words, one who lays claim to special privilege through the priesthood doesn't understand the nature of his authority. Priesthood is about service, not servitude; compassion, not compulsion; caring, not control. Those who think otherwise are operating outside the parameters of their authority and are gravely mistaken.

With that said, we are prepared to move ahead with our discussion of local Church councils. As we do so, we invoke the challenge of President Joseph F. Smith, who looked forward to the day "when every council of the Priesthood in the Church of Jesus Christ of Latter-day Saints will understand its duty; will assume its own responsibility, will magnify its calling, and fill its place in the Church, to the uttermost, according to the intelligence and ability possessed by it. . . . When they become thoroughly awakened to the requirements made of them, they will fulfil their duties more faithfully, and the work of the Lord will be all the stronger and more powerful and influential in the world" (in Conference Report, Apr. 1906, 3).

CHAPTER 3

LOCAL PRESIDING COUNCILS

In view of the accelerating growth of the Church and the ever-faster unraveling of society's moral and spiritual fabric throughout the world, it is increasingly imperative to empower leaders of stakes, wards, and homes to do whatever it takes, in harmony with gospel principles, to bring people to Christ. Every person and situation is unique in some way. While principles are universally applicable, practices are not. As every parent knows who has tried to rear the second child exactly like the first, what works in one situation may fail in another.

The central activity of leadership is teaching—first by example, second by precept. After that, leaders become a source of help as their empowered stewards assume the responsibility and exercise the initiative to do whatever is necessary, consistent with the principles taught, to fulfill the shared vision.

The most advanced, universal, and practical leadership philosophy ever put forth was given in this simple statement by the Prophet Joseph Smith: "I teach the people correct principles and they govern themselves" (quoted by John Taylor, in *Journal of Discourses*, 10:57-58). Area Presidencies are to teach stake presidencies the overall vision, direction, purpose, and correct principles of the Church, and then they are to let stake presidencies govern or manage their stakes. A similar pattern applies to bishops and their wards and to parents and their families. "Wherefore, now let every man learn his duty, and to act in the office in which he is appointed, in all diligence" (D&C 107:99).

This empowerment process requires leaders to exercise great patience while modeling Christlike behavior; building caring, trusting relationships; setting up clear role and goal expectations; identifying sources of help; and requiring accountability. Generally, Church leaders teach principles, not practices. Inspired stake, ward, and family council members learn to convert principles into appropriate practices through the whisperings of the Holy Ghost. For example, after teaching the principle of daily family prayer, a father may ask, "How and when should our family hold family prayer?" The family may determine to hold family prayer just before the children go to school. This may become a family practice for many years. Later, the family may find it more practical to hold family prayer in conjunction with the evening meal or at bedtime. Practices may change, but fundamental principles and purposes do not change.

As leaders work with their councils, careful attention should be given to this admonition from the Lord: "For behold, it is not meet that I should command in all things; for he that is compelled in all things, the same is a slothful and not a wise servant; wherefore he receiveth no reward. Verily I say, men should be anxiously engaged in a good cause, and *do many things of their own free will*, and bring to pass much righteousness; *for the power is in them*, wherein they are agents unto themselves" (D&C 58:26–28; emphasis added). When so empowered, council members will become amazingly creative and willing to take the initiative in doing whatever is necessary to accomplish worthy purposes within the guidelines of well-understood principles.

In addition to teaching purposes and principles, it is important that leaders explicitly teach what *not* to do, as the Lord did in several of the Ten Commandments. This leaves open every appropriate path to the creativeness of the council so that they can feel responsible and successfully achieve results rather than thinking, "Well, we did what we were told to do and it didn't work. Now what do they want us to do?"

UNANIMITY IN COUNCIL

One of the important principles governing leadership councils in The Church of Jesus Christ of Latter-day Saints is the principle of unanimity. Generally speaking, issues considered by presiding councils should be discussed and evaluated until a course of action is unanimously approved. In the Quorum of the Twelve Apostles, for example, decisions that lack unanimity are always held over for further thought, prayer, and discussion. Even though we have a President whom we respect and revere, and we are organized with a clear line of successive authority, we seek consensus in all that we do. As a result, there have been times when an issue has remained under consideration for a period of time while our decision was deliberated and fine-tuned. Eventually, consensus is achieved, and the result of our deliberation is a better and more complete decision.

Of course, it isn't always possible to take that kind of time with the decisions that face presidencies and bishoprics. Some issues require a quick response; and sometimes, even after an open discussion during which all ideas and perspectives are given a thorough airing, divergent and disparate views exist. At such times, it is the responsibility of the president or bishop to make a final decision based on the feelings and impressions that come through priesthood keys or the mantle of leadership. And it is the responsibility of all members of the presiding council to support and sustain the decision of the council leader as if it were a unanimous council decision.

President James E. Faust, speaking several years ago in the priesthood session of a general conference, emphasized the vital importance of this principle:

> There is a constant need for unity within the priesthood. We must be loyal to the leadership who have been called to preside over us and hold the keys of the priesthood. The words of President J. Reuben Clark, Jr., still ring loudly in our ears: *"Brethren, let us be united."* He explained:
>
> "An essential part of unity is loyalty. . . . Loyalty is a pretty difficult quality to possess. It requires the ability to put away selfishness, greed, ambition and all of the baser qualities of the human mind. You cannot be loyal unless you are willing to surrender. . . . [A person's] own preferences and desires must be put away, and he must see only the great purpose which lies out ahead" (*Immortality and Eternal Life*, Melchizedek Priesthood Course of Study, 1968–69, p. 163). . . .
>
> In some legislative assemblies of the world, there are some groups termed the "loyal opposition." I find no such principle in the gospel of Jesus Christ. The Savior gave us this solemn warning: "Be one; and if ye are not one ye are not mine" (D&C 38:27). The Lord made it clear that in the presiding quorums every decision "must be by the unanimous voice of the same; that is, every member in each quorum must be agreed to its decisions" (D&C 107:27). This means that after frank and open discussion, decisions are reached in council under the direction of the presiding officer, who has the ultimate authority to decide. That decision is then sustained, because our unity comes from full agreement with righteous principles and general response to the

operation of the Spirit of God. ("Keeping Covenants and Honoring the Priesthood," 36–38)

Soon after I was called to be a bishop, all of the bishops in our stake met with the stake presidency in what was then called a stake bishops' council. Back in those days, the bishops of the stake were asked to help create the stake's annual welfare budget, and we had been involved in that process for several meetings, giving our input and recommendations. Finally, the presidency presented to us a final budget proposal for our sustaining vote, and I was a little surprised when two of the bishops voted negatively due to some budgeted items with which they did not agree.

"Why don't you brethren give the matter some thought and prayer," our stake president suggested gently. "We'll take another vote in our next meeting."

At the next stake bishops' council meeting, another vote was taken to sustain the stake welfare budget. Once again, the two bishops voted in the negative. This time our stake president wasn't quite so gentle.

"Brethren, this is the welfare budget that we as your stake presidency feel comfortable with," he said firmly but gently. "We have listened to your recommendations and have done the best we could to implement your suggestions. And now we've reached a decision, one that we feel has been validated by the Spirit.

"The way I see it," the president continued, "either God is working through us or we are fallen leaders. That means that your choice here is simple: sustain us and this budget, or write a letter to the First Presidency and ask that we be released. Now, all in favor of sustaining the proposed stake welfare budget, please show it by the usual sign."

This time, every bishop in the council raised his hand in approval. Within a few months every bishop in that council could see the wisdom and inspiration behind the stake presidency's recommended budget.

The same principle holds true for smaller councils, including bishoprics and stake and ward auxiliary presidencies. Unanimity should always be sought through free and open discussion. When there is a difference of opinion and an immediate decision is not required, it is sometimes helpful to allow some time to pass to give council members a chance to think about the decision and perhaps come to a state of unanimity naturally. But when the time comes that a decision has to be made and a variance of opinion still exists, the council leader has to rely upon the Spirit and make the decision that he or she feels is best. At such times it is particularly important for all council members to support and sustain the decision of the council leader—even if it isn't a decision with which they personally agree—and have faith in the spirit of revelation as it moves upon the bishop or president. If we can't find unanimity in the specific decision, we can at least find unanimity in our support of our sustained leader and our desire to see the work of the Lord go forward in a positive, cooperative way. Although we have different viewpoints and opinions, when we emerge from counseling as a council we are one, and we support the final decision of the council as if it were our own, personal decision.

"Be of one mind," the Apostle Paul urged early Christian leaders in Corinth (2 Corinthians 13:11). And to the Saints at Philippi he wrote, "Only let your conversation be as it becometh the gospel of Christ . . . that ye stand fast in one spirit, with one mind striving together for the faith of the gospel" (Philippians 1:27). Through the Prophet Joseph Smith, the Lord counseled his latter-day followers to "be one; and if ye are not one ye are not mine" (D&C 38:27). In every council of the Church, but especially in stakes and wards, this divine counsel is profoundly important. If we are one in purpose, spirit, principle, and faith, then it doesn't really matter if we are always of the same opinion. Opinions change and can be easily altered by time, experience, and circumstance. But principles, purposes, spirituality, and faith are enduring values that can bind us as one despite disagreement or dispute.

CONFIDENTIALITY IN COUNCIL

Another important principle governing presiding councils in the Church is the principle of confidentiality. It would be difficult to exaggerate the importance of keeping council proceedings confidential. The Prophet Joseph Smith once said: "The reason we do not have the secrets of the Lord revealed unto us, is because we do not keep them but reveal them; we do not keep our own secrets, but reveal our difficulties to the world, even to our enemies, then how would we keep the secrets of the Lord? I can keep a secret till Doomsday" (*History of the Church,* 4:479).

One bishop learned firsthand how destructive it can be when council members are not careful to safeguard the things that are discussed in meetings. A council member inadvertently left a copy of the council agenda on a church bench. On the agenda were penciled notes about a family who had been targeted for the special attention of the council. It was found there by a teenage member of the family.

Imagine the effect such a careless thing had on the family members. Offended that they had been the subject of discussion by the leaders of the ward, the parents had their feelings hurt. Though the bishop and the members of the council had intended only to help, the damage that was done through carelessness made it difficult to break through the resulting family resentment and embarrassment.

Each council member is obligated to keep confidential the matters he or she discusses and hears. Members of presidencies and bishoprics are often entrusted with extremely sensitive matters, and they compromise their position of trust when they share such information inappropriately. Such breaches can have enormously destructive repercussions. One stake president made it a policy that high council members weren't to discuss council business outside of the council meeting—even among themselves. There is never any reason for council members to share with others (including their spouses) details of the business of the council, particularly with regard to individual needs or differences of opinion. If we are to bless people's lives and avoid hurting them, we simply must learn to keep confidential things confidential.

THE VALUE OF LISTENING IN COUNCIL

The presidents and bishops who utilize Church councils most effectively are those who do a lot of listening in council meetings. If you're the presiding officer, that doesn't mean that you just sit there quietly. It means that you really listen to what your counselors and other council members are saying and feeling, and that you ask meaningful, penetrating questions when you don't understand their perspective. While it is true that final decisions and directions rest with the person who has been called to preside, there is little reason to have council members with unique insights, experiences, and abilities if you're not going to pay attention to what they have to say. Let your council members know that you value their input and that you expect them to express themselves. Since the presiding officer sets the tone in each meeting, it is up to you to make sure that those who serve under your direction feel that their participation is welcome. It is usually helpful to hear other opinions before offering your own. Too often, when a leader expresses his or her opinion first, the discussions conclude prematurely.

"Let not all be spokesmen at once," the Lord said, "but let one speak at a time and let all listen unto his sayings, that when all have spoken that all may be edified of all, and that every man may have an equal privilege" (D&C 88:122).

At the same time, one who is called to serve on a Church council should remember that his or her participation on the council is a privilege. And with that privilege comes responsibility—responsibility to work within the parameters of the organization, to be prepared, to share, to advocate vigorously the position he or she believes to be right. But just as important is the responsibility to support and sustain the final decision of the council leader.

Furthermore, each council member has a responsibility to be spiritually in tune when taking part in council meetings so that he or she can make a positive contribution to the issues being discussed. For example, the Prophet Joseph Smith taught that "every man, before he makes an objection to any item that is brought before a council for consideration, should be sure that he can throw light upon the subject rather than spread darkness, and that his objection be founded in righteousness, which may be done by men applying themselves closely to study the mind and will of the Lord, whose Spirit always makes manifest and demonstrates the truth to the understanding of all who are in possession of the Spirit" (*History of the Church,* 2:370). As we do this, our councils will be conducted in a spirit of love and compassion and will follow the example of the Lord, who "counseleth in wisdom, and in justice, and in great mercy" (Jacob 4:10).

By listening to council members, presidents and bishops can share with other leaders the burdens they have been called to bear. We have already noted the counsel of a good, righteous father in Israel named Jethro to his son-in-law, Moses. When Jethro visited Moses, he watched as he

sat to judge the people: and the people stood by Moses from the morning unto the evening.

And when Moses' father in law saw all that he did to the people, he said, What is this thing that thou doest to the people? why sittest thou thyself alone, and all the people stand by thee from morning unto even?

And Moses said unto his father in law, Because the people come unto me to enquire of God:

When they have a matter, they come unto me; and I judge between one and another, and I do make them know the statues of God, and his laws.

And Moses' father in law said unto him, The thing that thou doest is not good.

Thou wilt surely wear away, both thou, and this people that is with thee: for this thing is too heavy for thee; thou art not able to perform it thyself alone.

Hearken now unto my voice, I will give thee counsel, and God shall be with thee: Be thou for the people to God-ward, that thou mayest bring the causes unto God:

And thou shalt teach them ordinances and laws, and shalt shew them the way wherein they must walk, and the work that they must do.

Moreover thou shalt provide out of all the people able men, such as fear God, men of truth, hating covetousness; and place such over them, to be rulers of thousands, and rulers of hundreds, rulers of fifties, and rulers of tens:

And let them judge the people at all seasons: and it shall be, that every great matter they shall bring unto thee, but every small matter they shall judge: so shall it be easier for thyself, and they shall bear the burden with thee.

If thou shalt do this thing, and God command thee so, then thou shalt be able to endure, and all this people shall also go to their place in peace. (Exodus 18:13–23)

Not only is this a great lesson for all of us on the importance of delegation of priesthood authority, but it also illustrates the need for presidents and bishops to allow their counselors, auxiliary leaders, and other associates to "bear the burden with thee." Remember, presidents and bishops, that the callings of your associates are just as divinely inspired as is yours, and they are therefore entitled to inspiration in their specific responsibilities. Lean upon them. Learn from them. Love them. Listen to them.

COUNCIL LEADERSHIP

I would also offer this suggestion to presidents and bishops: Never forget that as the council leader, you are ultimately responsible for all decisions. Now, that may seem contradictory to our previous discussion on the importance of listening to the counsel of other council members. But it isn't—not at all. Rather, it is a natural extension of the flow of council leadership in the Church. The ideal model is straightforward and simple: call good people to serve with you, listen carefully to their counsel and consider their input, and then listen to the whisperings of the Holy Spirit as it leads you to make good decisions. Functioning successfully as a council doesn't mean making group decisions. It simply means the council leader draws from the various abilities, insights, experiences, and inspiration of council members to help make good decisions under the influence of the Spirit. While we seek unanimity, the final decision is always up to the council leader.

One bishop told me of a time soon after his call to the bishopric when a new Young Women president was needed in his ward. "There was a clear impression in my mind who the new president should be," the bishop said. "But when I spoke with my counselors about the call, they had another name in mind, and they made a good and compelling case for the second woman to serve in this important position.

"I was a brand-new bishop, and I had tremendous respect for these two good men who were serving as my counselors," the bishop continued. "I guess I had more confidence in them than I did in my own spiritual sensitivity, because I chose to ignore what I was personally feeling and to accept their recommendation as the decision of the council."

The bishop was unable to issue the call before he had to leave town for an extended business trip, so he asked his first counselor to extend the call to the second woman. When he called a couple of days later to ask his counselor how things were going, he was told that there had been a problem. The woman, a faithful and devoted young sister, felt uncomfortable with the calling and asked for a day or two to reconcile her feelings.

"It just doesn't feel right," she said after a couple of prayerful days. "I've never declined a calling in my life, and I won't decline this one. But I feel that I need to ask you to ask the bishop if he's really sure that this is what the Lord wants for the young women of the ward right now. If it is, then I'll assume that the problem here is mine and I'll willingly accept the assignment."

"Of course she feels uncomfortable," the bishop said when his counselor explained the situation. "This isn't what the Lord wants. He let me know who the new Young Women president is supposed to be, and I've been ignoring Him."

The bishop instructed his counselor to let the sister know that there was nothing wrong with her spiritual sensitivity. Then he was to go ahead and extend the calling to the sister the bishop had been originally impressed to call.

Her response was validating: "I've had the impression for two weeks that this calling was coming."

"The experience didn't teach me to ignore my counselors," the bishop said. "Their input was important—the woman they suggested was called to serve as a Young Women adviser, and she did a wonderful job there. But I did learn that of all the voices I was to listen to as bishop, the most important one was the voice of the Spirit as it guided my thoughts, my words, and my actions."

It is important that all council members understand the significant and very distinct role of the council leader and learn to not be offended when the decision is different from the course they would have chosen. Decision making isn't the primary responsibility of counselors. Counselors are called to do just that—to provide counsel—as well as to assist, strengthen, and support. Their role is to participate—actively and candidly—in the decision-making process, to support and sustain all council decisions, and to execute their implementation through their respective organizations.

USING COUNCILS TO ACCOMPLISH THE MISSION OF THE CHURCH

Of course, the fundamental guiding principle of every Church council is to accomplish the mission of the Church. Everything discussed, every plan made, every activity coordinated should have as its central focus bringing souls to Christ by either proclaiming the gospel, perfecting the Saints, or redeeming the dead—or a combination of the three. If an agenda item can't logically and naturally be linked to one of those great and wonderful eternal pursuits—without having to be stretched beyond recognition in order to fit—then perhaps it does not belong on the agenda.

From time to time, the First Presidency and the Quorum of the Twelve Apostles will place special emphasis on the fundamental principles of the gospel to help train leaders in accomplishing the mission of the Church. All Church councils need to be aware of and ready to support any new point of emphasis from the First Presidency and the Quorum of the Twelve. My guess is that many council leaders and members will be surprised to discover how much more focused their work will become when they examine it through the lens of saving souls through the mission of the Church.

One young bishop I know was taught this important concept by a good stake president. "I had been serving as bishop for about a year," he told me. "I had great counselors, and we all were working hard and expending a lot of time and energy in our callings. We had lots of great activities, and our meetings were always well planned and executed. We were doing all of the things that we thought we were supposed to be doing, but we didn't seem to be accomplishing anything of real, lasting significance in the lives of the members of our ward. We were so busy being busy that we never had time to focus on things that really mattered. Very few less-active members' lives were being touched, no prospective elders were being advanced to the Melchizedek Priesthood, our young men were not going on missions, and no one could remember when we had last baptized a convert into the Church in our ward."

Sound familiar? Most of us have been there. Church callings are demanding, particularly if you're serving in a presidency or a bishopric. There is much to do, and there are many details to arrange. Sometimes we get so focused on bringing people to the meetinghouse that we forget we are supposed to be bringing them to Christ. Too often, our council meetings reflect that lack of focus. We find ourselves spending all of our precious time during council meetings coordinating events and correlating schedules. Instead of doing the Lord's business—which almost always has to do with touching the lives of individuals and families—we allow ourselves to get bogged down in administrative busyness. Reports are submitted and assignments are made and the meeting is considered a success, even though there has been no serious discussion of how to move the organization forward in proclaiming the gospel, perfecting the Saints, and redeeming the dead—each of which involves touching and influencing people.

71

It's no wonder, then, that many presidents and bishops presiding over such organizations feel overwhelmed and unfulfilled, as my young friend did. If your calling has become simply a long list of things that need to be done—activities that need to be planned, lessons that need to be prepared, assignments that need to be filled, meetings that need to be held—it can be daunting. It is only when we get beyond the administrative details of our callings and focus our attention on the principles of ministering to God's children and bringing the blessings of the gospel into their lives that our Church offices take on their full meaning, and we experience the fulfilling joy and satisfaction to be found in rendering significant service in the kingdom.

For example, a carefully planned sacrament meeting should be a spiritual feast in which we worship and learn of our Heavenly Father and His Beloved Son, our Lord and Savior, Jesus Christ. Surely once each week our members should feel the power of the Spirit in their lives. Sacrament meeting should provide such an opportunity. Bishops who are bogged down in details often find themselves spending more time on insignificant matters and less time on ensuring that sacrament meetings are a banquet of spiritual nourishment. At such times, it would be wise to invite suggestions from counselors and ward council members on ways to make every sacrament meeting a more reverent, spiritual experience. Let the councils also help teach our members that the chapel is a special place in our buildings where we come in a spirit of respect for God and reverence for His Holy Son. I am sure that if invited by the bishop, the auxiliary presidents could teach in their meetings the need to improve reverence in sacrament meeting. The sisters can teach each other and their families that the chapel is a special place, the only place where we can worship and honor the Lord Jesus Christ by partaking of the sacrament and renewing our covenants with Him. All leaders can help the quiet, peaceful promptings of the Holy Spirit abide in our worship services, causing spiritual enlightenment and nourishment to flow into our lives. By focusing attention on such issues that stem directly from our efforts to accomplish the mission of the Church, presiding councils shift their vision from *administration* to *ministration,* and the council members experience the joy that comes from making a meaningful difference in people's lives.

Fortunately, that well-intentioned-but-frustrated-and-slightly-harried bishop we mentioned earlier had an insightful stake president who understood that principle.

"Do you have a copy of one of your bishopric meeting agendas?" the president asked during one of their regular personal priesthood interviews. When the agenda was produced, the president studied it for a moment, then put it down on his desk. "When do you talk about the spiritual needs of your people?" he asked.

My friend was surprised by the question. "Well," he said, "we talk about that all the time."

The stake president glanced at the agenda. "I don't see it on here," he observed.

"Maybe it isn't an agenda item, but we do talk about it," the bishop said.

"Give me an example," the president pressed.

Now it was my friend's turn to study the agenda. "Right here," he said at last, pointing to an agenda item labeled *New Callings.* "We talked about calling some new teachers in Primary and Relief Society." The bishop paused uncomfortably, then added: "I remember we talked about how important it was to call good teachers."

"Well, that's fine," the stake president said. "But I'm still curious to know why you don't talk specifically about the spiritual needs of your members. Remember, Bishop, proclaiming the gospel, perfecting the Saints, and redeeming the dead are guidelines to help us lift our people spiritually and, in doing so, strengthen the Church."

"Yes, President, I know," the bishop said. "And we do talk about them. We just don't have them on our agenda."

"I see that," the president said, "and I guess I'm wondering why. What I do see on your agenda are a lot of maintenance tasks: new callings, stake announcements, interview lists, activities reports, calendaring. With everything you've got to go through here, any discussion of items related to meeting spiritual needs would be purely incidental, or would be left until late in the meeting when there isn't time to explore those issues in the depth they deserve."

The bishop looked down at his agenda again. He noticed the last item on the agenda—*Activation*—and recalled how often they hadn't had time to hold that important discussion. "I think I see your point, President," he said. "But I'm not exactly sure what to do about it. I mean, those maintenance items do need to be handled."

"Of course they do," the president said. "But they don't have to be the central focus of your bishopric meeting." He paused to pull a form out of his desk. "Here," he said, "look at our last stake presidency meeting agenda." The bishop saw that following the opening prayer and scriptural thought, the minutes, and reports on assignments, the agenda was then divided into three sections—Proclaiming the Gospel, Perfecting the Saints, and Redeeming the Dead—with specific items for discussion listed under each heading. Upon closer inspection, he noticed that there were a number of specific names listed on the agenda, and not a lot of detail management.

"How do you do that?" he asked. "The stake seems to run smoothly and efficiently. How do you keep things going without spending time working through details and plans?"

"We do," the president responded. "But we handle those matters quickly during a reporting period at the beginning of the meeting. And we do a lot of maintenance outside of presidency meeting. Our objective is to focus as much time as possible in our meetings on the things that really matter. And the things that really matter almost always have to do with people— their needs, their concerns, their faith, and how they relate to the spiritual strength of the Church."

My young friend caught the vision of his stake president's wise counsel and began reshaping his bishopric meeting agendas according to the spiritual and personal needs of ward members. "At first," he said, "it felt a little funny to spend so much time talking about people's needs and other weighty issues, and we weren't as organized as we used to be. But now, we've figured out how to conduct the business of the ward without spending all of our time in bishopric meeting talking about it. And we find that we're much more intimately involved in people's lives, and better able to make a difference through applying fundamental principles of the gospel in the lives of our people to help lift them spiritually."

What he learned through that experience applies to every bishopric, every presidency, and every council in the Church. Maintaining that critical focus in meetings and in ministering to the needs of the people is one of the most important things a president or bishop can do. As the presiding authority of the council, he or she sets the ministerial tone that others throughout the organization will follow. Presidency or bishopric meeting is the perfect place to establish a clear focus on the principal thing that should matter most to all Church councils: bringing souls to Christ and securing them with spiritual witness and testimony.

Every council must choose between the things that really matter and the things that don't. It is the responsibility of counselors and other council members to help the president or bishop or auxiliary leader stay focused on the things that matter: the spiritual progress of every person living within that unit of the Church. If we spend all of our time talking about trivia, then our work will be trivial. But this is God's work, and it is anything but trivial. If we stay focused and keep our objectives clear, we can work through our councils to move forward the mission of the Church in our stakes, wards, quorums, and auxiliaries.

LEADERSHIP TRAINING EMPHASIS

To help priesthood and auxiliary leaders focus their efforts on accomplishing the mission of the Church, the First Presidency and the Quorum of the Twelve Apostles have issued a document entitled "Leadership Training Emphasis," which contains the following guidelines:

Families: Teach the preeminence of the home and family as the basic organizational unit of the Church. Encourage each family member, parents and children, to study the scriptures, pray regularly, and follow the example of the Savior in all things.

Adults: Encourage each adult to be worthy to receive the ordinances of the temple. Teach all adults to identify their ancestors and perform sacred temple ordinances for them.

Youth: Help prepare each young man to receive the Melchizedek Priesthood, to receive the ordinances of the temple, and to be worthy to serve a full-time mission. Help prepare each young woman to be worthy to make and keep sacred covenants and receive the ordinances of the temple.

All Members: Leaders, members, and stake and full-time missionaries work cooperatively in a balanced effort to help convert, retain, and activate our Heavenly Father's children. Teach members to provide for themselves, their families, and the poor and needy in the Lord's way.

These are the things that matter. These are the things that will make a positive difference in people's lives. And these are the things that should be the focus and objective of every presiding council in the Church as we seek to join the Lord in His work and His glory—"to bring to pass the immortality and eternal life of man" (Moses 1:39).

CHAPTER 4

STAKE AND DISTRICT COUNCILS

A friend whom I'll call Brent was a little discouraged with his new Church calling. For most of the previous year he had held what he referred to as "the best calling in the Church": Sunday School teacher for a group of inquisitive, enthusiastic, and well-behaved sixteen- and seventeen-year-olds. They had enjoyed wonderful times together, filled with some rather unique gospel insights, lots of laughter, and occasional tears. The group had bonded in a meaningful way, and when the Sunday School president told Brent that they didn't want to stop the spiritual momentum that was building with the class and were going to keep him with the group for the next year, he was thrilled.

That's why he was a little concerned when the new bishop in his ward asked Brent and his wife to come for an interview. Since his wife was already serving as Relief Society president, they figured it was not going to be a new calling for her. So Brent wasn't too surprised when the bishop extended a new calling to him: Young Men president.

"I was disappointed at first," Brent admitted. "I didn't want to leave that class. But since the Young Men president is also the priests quorum adviser, I would still be with all of the young men who were in the Sunday School class, and I'd be able to associate with the young women at Mutual, so it didn't take long for me to get used to the idea. In fact, I was pretty excited about it by the time stake conference rolled around the next week."

Ah, yes, stake conference—in this case, a special stake conference in which Brent's stake was divided and a lot of reorganization took place. By the end of the conference, Brent's one-week stint as ward Young Men president was over and he was a member of a new stake high council. And that's where his discouragement came in.

"It isn't the quick change that bothers me—I understand that things like that happen in a growing, dynamic Church," Brent told me. "It's just . . . you know, a *stake* assignment."

I understood what he was trying to say. We had talked about it before, when he had served as a member of another high council. When I first met Brent he was a bishop, and he loved serving at the ward level because of its proximity to people and the opportunity it gave him to get involved in a meaningful way in their lives.

"You can really minister to people in a ward assignment—you can make a difference in their lives," he said. "Stake assignments are just . . . well, administrative. You shuffle papers. You handle details. You go to meetings—*lots* of meetings. But you don't really *do* anything. I mean, when was the last time you heard someone say that their life was changed by a high council speaker?"

Many who have served in stake assignments can probably relate to what my friend Brent was saying. The impact of effective service tends to be more immediate, more clearly seen, and more personally felt in ward callings than in stake callings. In ward callings, we minister to people; in stake callings, we teach and minister to those who minister. But that ministry can be just as important—and, in the long term, just as profound—if we take our stake assignments seriously and bring to them the same determination and dedication that we would bring to a ward assignment. The stake Young Women leader who can help her ward counterpart better understand the program and be more effective in her service, who can give her a vision of the impact of her calling, is blessing the lives of young women just as surely as the ward leader is; she's just doing it indirectly. To help a teacher or adviser be more effective in reaching the youth in the ward is truly a great service. Similarly, the high councilor who devotes his time to providing excellent training and instruction in stake training meetings is rendering a valuable service to those whose lives are enriched as a result of that training. While it is sometimes more difficult to see the long-term results of our work in stake assignments, the service can be every bit as satisfying and joyful for those who understand and see the necessity of ministering to those who minister.

The aims and objectives of stake councils are slightly different from those of the equivalent ward councils (where such equivalency exists), but the principles that should govern these councils are identical. It is just as important to focus on gospel fundamentals and on people (rather than programs) in stake councils as it is in ward councils, and it is just as important that those who participate in stake councils be able to do so in a spirit of free and open discussion. The principles of counseling with our councils are true whether we are talking about a stake council or a ward council, and the results of doing so effectively can be just as significant in the lives of individuals and families.

While there can be any number of ad hoc stake councils and committees, for the purposes of our discussion we will focus our attention on three standing councils at the stake level.

The *stake priesthood executive committee* consists of the stake presidency and the high council. The stake priesthood executive committee meeting, often called "high council meeting," is held at least twice monthly (where feasible) to consider stake priesthood and auxiliary matters. The stake president presides and conducts; the stake executive secretary and the stake clerk also attend this meeting. The stake Melchizedek Priesthood committee and the stake Aaronic Priesthood committee are subcommittees of the stake priesthood executive committee.

The *stake welfare committee* is formed by adding the stake Relief Society presidency and the chairman of the stake bishops' welfare council to the stake priesthood executive committee. This committee meets at least quarterly to coordinate stake welfare services and activities.

The *stake council* includes stake priesthood executive committee members, the stake mission president, and the presidents of the stake auxiliaries. The stake president may also invite others to attend as needed. Although some stakes continue to refer to this body as the "stake correlation council," it is correctly referred to as the stake council, for its scope and vision should extend far beyond mere correlation and coordination of activities. While planning and coordinating are key functions of stake council members, this group should also consider key issues, needs, and concerns confronting those who live within stake boundaries.

BLESSING LIVES THROUGH STAKE COUNCILS

In one stake, such an issue was temple attendance by stake members. Stake leaders were concerned because they believed that members were not taking full advantage of the opportunity to have the blessings of temple worship in their lives. The stake presidency spoke about their shared concern at length, and they tried to communicate it through meetings and conferences. But they had not put the issue before the stake council.

"Our stake council meetings had never been very useful,"

the stake president admitted. "They were more calendaring get-togethers than anything else. We scheduled only two stake council meetings each year, mostly because the handbook said we should hold regular council meetings. Two seemed like more than enough as far as we were concerned."

But after watching a training video about stake and ward councils and hearing some strong counsel from general Church leaders about how to effectively counsel with our councils, the stake presidency decided to use a different approach with their stake council. "At our next council meeting we showed part of the training video and then discussed the purpose of holding this particular meeting," the stake president said. "We made it clear that this was not a calendaring meeting, but a meeting that would help the stake move forward in accomplishing the mission of the Church: to proclaim the gospel, to perfect the Saints, and to redeem the dead."

Then the stake presidency presented their concern about temple attendance to the stake council and asked for their comments and suggestions. "The Spirit was with us, and the ideas just flowed," the stake president said. "The sisters who were present were particularly helpful in offering suggestions about how to make temple attendance more convenient for working women and mothers with small children at home."

"It was a positive time for everyone attending," he continued. "There was a great deal of participation, because all council members felt that they were being listened to and that their suggestions were being considered."

The council meeting generated a lengthy list of ideas, some of which eventually became the stake's plan for increasing temple attendance. "But the really exceptional outcome was that everyone said we should hold stake council meetings more often," the stake president said. "Now that we've figured out how to take advantage of the collective expertise of our stake council, we're scheduling stake council meetings quarterly, with provisions to meet more often if needed. We need what the stake council can do for us—now that we know how to use it."

A similar experience occurred in another stake, where stake council meetings had been eliminated altogether and replaced by regular meetings between the stake presidency and individual stake auxiliary presidencies. As a result of counsel from Church leaders, the stake president and his counselors decided to reconstitute and reschedule the stake council.

"In the first of these meetings we discussed the outlines of both ward and stake conferences, among other items," the stake president said. "The comments and suggestions from stake council members were critical in shaping our ward and stake conference agendas. And as it turned out, our ward and stake conferences were among the most successful we've ever had. Comments from our members on the last two stake conferences have been extremely positive, and in both cases attendance has been up."

"We also found that in revising our format for ward conferences, we were coming much closer to meeting the needs of both the leadership and the individual members," the stake president continued. "Further, we increased the involvement of the sisters in the ward conferences, and this has been met with a very positive response."

Another stake president learned in an area priesthood training meeting how strongly the First Presidency and the Quorum of the Twelve Apostles felt about the bearing of testimony and the teaching of pure doctrine in all Church meetings to elevate the spirituality of individual members. The Area Presidency explained the "Leadership Training Emphasis" document (see Chapter 3) and asked the stake presidents to focus on preparing all of their people to receive the blessings of the temple. The stake president returned to his stake determined to find a way to emphasize the message in each of the wards. First he counseled with his counselors, and together they determined that the principles taught in the "Leadership Training Emphasis" document needed to be understood and taught in their stake. Then he held an expanded stake council meeting, adding all of the ward bishops, in which he and his counselors presented the information. In this meeting, the council members discussed ways to implement the instruction from the Brethren throughout the stake.

Each bishop met with his ward council to determine how to act upon the stake presidency's message. The stake auxiliary presidents counseled with their respective organizations as well. For example, the stake Relief Society presidency came up with a plan that included teaching these principles to ward Relief Society presidents at stake leadership meetings, incorporating the theme into the annual stake women's conference, encouraging Relief Society teachers to more effectively teach doctrine and bear testimony, doing further training with ward presidents on a one-on-one basis, and suggesting ways to incorporate the message in meaningful homemaking activities.

"For the first time, we felt that we were part of the stake leadership team," said the stake Relief Society president. "It was exhilarating to be regarded as spiritual leaders who could help contribute to the overall spirituality of our stake."

MAKING STAKE COUNCILS WORK

Do you see a pattern in these examples of effective stake councils? It seems that there are three keys to making stake councils work in the way they were designed and intended to work. First, beginning with the stake presidency, stake leadership must be committed to the council concept and to doing everything in their power to see that the councils are formed and operating as they should. Second, they must empower their councils; that is, give council members meaningful work to do. And finally, they have to get out of the way and allow the stake council to function.

A stake president tells of discussing an upcoming temple preparation seminar with his stake priesthood executive committee. "As a stake presidency, we went into the meeting and told the brethren how the seminar should be handled. They just sat there, listening to us, without any expressions of support or excitement."

The presidency was concerned, and in their next presidency meeting they counseled together on how the stake priesthood executive committee could be improved. "It occurred to us that we had the habit of telling the high council how we were going to do things, as opposed to counseling with them and receiving their ideas and input," the stake president said. "At our next priesthood executive committee meeting we approached the temple preparation seminar in a different way. We asked for their suggestions and recommendations, and then we sat back and waited for them to respond. At first they were hesitant—this was a new way of doing things. But soon momentum began to build and the ideas began to flow. There was a good spirit there, and some great ideas were presented that improved our temple preparation seminar plans.

"After the meeting, one of the brethren came up to me and said, 'This is one of the most productive meetings I have ever attended. It felt good to be here. Thank you.'"

Too often in the Church we take productive priesthood leaders and put them on high councils where their perceived role is simply to give rubber-stamp approval to stake presidency plans and programs and to run ecclesiastical errands for the presiding brethren. Under such conditions, high councilors quickly become "dry" councilors; without the spiritual nourishment of meaningful service, they lose enthusiasm, energy, and commitment to the work. Similarly, talented and spiritually gifted women called as auxiliary leaders are too often treated by priesthood leaders as though their only function is to take in casseroles and arrange for stake and ward activities. The fact is that they are spiritual leaders who should be encouraged to actively contribute, under the direction of the priesthood, to the spiritual leadership of the ward, stake, or home. When stake presidencies allow stake councils to feel some ownership of the program, they are more likely to become a dynamic part of the solution to the problems facing the stake.

Inspired Leadership by a High Councilor

I had an experience some time ago in Idaho when I attended a stake conference there. The stake president mentioned he had a surprise for me and asked, "Will you trust me?" I responded, "Well, we trust all of our stake presidents; I trust you if you are right." He said, "Well, I think you will enjoy what is going to happen tomorrow in the general session of the conference."

Here is what happened. In the Sunday morning session, he called upon a little girl who was about ten years of age to come up to the pulpit and bear her testimony about being a "Primary missionary." What had happened was that the stake president had authorized the high council adviser to the Primary to implement an idea that children can also be missionaries. This high councilor went to the ward Primaries to teach the little children that they were missionaries too. This sweet little girl, whom we shall call Katie, learned from the high councilor that she could be a missionary. She came home to her father, who was the bishop of one of the wards, and said, "Daddy, I'm a Primary missionary, and I want to share the gospel with somebody." The bishop said, "Well, sweetheart, that's a wonderful thing, but we have only one or two nonmember families in our whole ward, so it might be a little difficult." But this little girl asked, "Who are they?" The bishop named the nonmember families, and his daughter promptly responded, "Let's you and me go visit them, and we'll invite them to come to our home for family home evening."

Those of you who are fathers of little girls know how easily you succumb when a sweet daughter looks at you imploringly out of innocent, trusting eyes. And that's what happened to the bishop. So he and Katie went and knocked on the door of one nonmember family. When the mother of the family answered the door, little Katie said, "I am a Primary missionary, and we want you to come to our house for family home evening." This wonderful mother, I guess, had the same problem with those big, innocent eyes, and she agreed to bring her family to home evening. They came; they had a nice evening; they were not converted.

About two weeks later, Katie came home just as her mother was taking some banana bread out of the oven. Katie asked, "Can I have a loaf of that bread?" Her mother said, "Yes sweetheart, but what do you want it for?"

"I want to take it to Mrs. Johnson," she replied.

When Mrs. Johnson came to the door, Katie said, "I have something for you that I would like to give you, but I can only give it to you on one condition." When Mrs. Johnson asked what the condition was, Katie responded, "That you let the missionaries teach you the gospel." Mrs. Johnson smiled and said, "If that's the only condition for us to have the banana bread, then I'll agree that we will let the missionaries teach us the gospel."

The missionaries taught the gospel to the Johnsons, and they were baptized.

After Katie finished her testimony at the conference, Sister Johnson was the next to speak. I shall never forget what I felt when she thanked a little ten-year-old Primary missionary who had had the courage to invite her family to learn about the gospel.

When it was my turn to speak, I invited the bishop and his family, including Katie, to come up and stand by me, and then I invited the Johnson family to come up—mother, father, and three children. I said to them, "You have had a wonderful experience together. Bishop, you and Katie have shared with your neighbor the most precious thing in life, the gospel of Jesus Christ. But I want to tell you that if you think your heart is filled with joy today, wait till that day one year from now when the Johnson family kneels at the altar in the Idaho Falls Temple to be sealed for time and all eternity. That will be a moment in mortality that you will never, ever forget."

One year later, I performed their sealing. When I walked into the temple, there in the waiting room was Katie, now age eleven, the Primary missionary. She was not able to go to the sealing room because she wasn't old enough, but she was there waiting for her convert family to be sealed. The sealing room was filled with members of the ward. When the three Johnson children knelt around that altar and I sealed them to their parents, it was a bit of heaven on earth—all made possible because a little girl took seriously an assignment from an inspired and motivated high councilor who had the idea that children could be missionaries too and who taught little Katie that she could share the gospel with others.

SPECIALIZED TASK COMMITTEES

Some of the best and most interesting council work being done in stakes and wards is performed by special task committees created to deal with specific issues and concerns. For example, one stake presidency was faced with a dilemma: of the sixty or so young single adults who lived within the stake boundaries, only about forty wanted to attend the stake's young single adult branch. Some were hopping from ward to ward with no accountability anywhere. The rest were attending other singles units in a large metropolitan area.

"In some cases, we weren't exactly sure where they were attending," the stake president said. "That was the problem. We wanted to make sure no one was falling through the cracks, and we wanted to provide a meaningful program for those who did not wish to attend the branch."

So, under the direction of the stake council, a special task committee was formed, composed of the stake Relief Society, Young Women, and Young Men presidents; four high councilors (whose respective responsibilities included the stake Young Men, Young Women, singles, and Relief Society organizations); the branch president and the elders quorum and Relief Society presidents from the young single adult branch; and the stake presidency. During their first meeting, the problem was outlined and all task committee members were asked to share their thoughts, impressions, and observations about the branch. The group also discussed current branch membership, potential branch membership, and the names of the young people who would be eligible to join the branch during the next four years.

"I was impressed that there was information being shared in that group that had never been discussed before," the stake president said. "There were situations and insights discussed that the task committee members had never been given an opportunity to express—especially among the sisters who were present. We knew we had a problem, but we had no idea of its shape or size until we convened that special committee. Immediately it became clear to us that our ward Relief Society organizations didn't know how to serve eighteen-year-old sisters who were out of high school but were too young to attend the singles branch. We had parents who were frustrated because they were watching as their young adults were losing interest in the Church, and they felt powerless to stop the trend. We had bishops who were pushing young adults out of their home wards, whether they wanted to attend the singles branch or not. And we had young people who weren't interested in the singles branch and really wanted to attend their home wards, but didn't feel there was anything for them there."

As a result of the discussion, assignments were made to

begin responding to some of the stake's greatest needs. First, all task committee members were asked to review the Church's official program for single adults to determine whether the stake was out of alignment with the Church. All of the bishops and ward Relief Society presidents were surveyed to find out what they were doing in their respective wards with regard to the young single adults. The information compiled by the task committee was presented to the stake council, where more candid and open dialogue led to the formation of a plan that was completely in line with the Church singles program.

"By returning to the Church program, we had to change some of our own long-entrenched ways of doing things, and that was painful to a degree," the stake president said. "I met again with the singles branch president and reviewed with him what we felt the Lord would have us do. We resolved his concerns and knelt in prayer, and within days there was complete support from him."

The proposed plan was then presented to the stake bishops' council for their sustaining vote. Concerns and reservations were voiced and then resolved as they counseled together, and the bishops sustained the stake presidency and began to implement the approved program.

The stake president said, "In our case, the task committee and stake council recommended that the single adults attend their home wards for Sunday meetings. Home ward bishops were committed to finding meaningful callings for every single adult. The stake would accelerate single adult activities and would encourage some multistake activities. All young single adults were also encouraged to attend institute classes. Each task committee and stake council member who participated in the process now has a personal commitment to the singles program and is anxious to see that it succeeds. We aren't doing this because the stake president decided that this is the way it should be; we're doing it because all who struggled with the challenges involved received his or her own testimony that in our stake this is what the Lord would have us do."

USING COUNCILS TO ADDRESS STAKE NEEDS

Try as I might, I can't think of any problem or concern faced by any stake of Zion that couldn't be similarly addressed through counseling with stake councils. When the presidency of one stake decided there was a need to improve respect for Church buildings and to increase reverence in meetings, the stake president and his counselors presented the matter to their stake council. "The meeting became a brainstorming session, and the ideas flowed," the stake president said. Among the suggestions that came from that first council meeting were the following: a theme, "Respect for Our Buildings"; sacrament meeting talks by high councilors on the subject; specific counsel to parents of young children, urging them to be selective in choosing the foods they bring into Church buildings for their little ones and asking them to teach their children the concepts of reverence and respect; messages for ward bulletins; and instructions to bishops to focus on reverence and respect in their wards in other ways.

Assignments were made, and stake council members went to work. High councilors began to prepare their messages. The stake executive secretary informed bishops of the important role they would play in emphasizing reverence and respect in their respective wards. A high councilor contacted all ward bulletin editors to carry reminders of respect and reverence in their programs. The stake Young Men president approached Aaronic Priesthood advisers and asked them to encourage their Young Men to accept responsibility for keeping the buildings clean on Sunday. The stake Primary president encouraged ward Primary leaders to teach reverence and respect in Primary sharing times. Young Women and Relief Society presidencies were also asked to work with their sisters in developing a greater understanding of what reverence really means.

"The results of the stake council's work have been very gratifying," the stake president said. "Reverence has increased. Respect for our buildings is highly visible. Members, both children and adults, are responding to the council's efforts to teach reverence and respect."

In another stake, the stake Melchizedek Priesthood committee played a pivotal role in updating the stake's emergency preparedness plan and broadening the scope of the plan to encourage greater community involvement, including those from other faiths. Committee members conducted training sessions, coordinated certification of volunteers through the local fire department's Community Emergency Response Team, and initiated contact with other area churches and organizations to solicit their involvement and support.

"The ideas, direction, and energy behind these efforts have been the result of the group synergy and inspiration that has occurred in the council meetings of our Melchizedek Priesthood committee," said the stake president. "This has been, for us, a very effective tool in accomplishing a number of objectives in our stake."

This is exactly what every stake council could be and should be—an effective tool in the hands of those who "minister to those who minister" in accomplishing the objectives of the stake and the mission of the Church.

INVOLVING ALL COUNCIL MEMBERS, BOTH MEN AND WOMEN

A wise stake president or bishop will see his auxiliary presidents as spiritual leaders rather than as organizers and party planners. Too many women leaders are underutilized and unappreciated, at times because priesthood leaders don't have a clear understanding or an enlightened view of the significant contribution the sisters can make. They too bear the mantle of presidency, and they have been set apart and blessed to assist the priesthood in bringing women and their families to Christ. In addition, faithful and devoted women are typically very receptive to the Spirit and can play unparalleled roles in helping foster spirituality among women, children, and youth.

President Boyd K. Packer of the Quorum of the Twelve Apostles, speaking several years ago in a general conference, emphasized the need for faithful and inspired women to make their influence felt within the Church:

> We need women who will applaud decency and quality in everything from the fashion of clothing to crucial social issues. We need women who are organized and women who can organize. We need women with executive ability who can plan and direct and administer; women who can teach, women who can speak out. There is a great need for women who can receive inspiration to guide them personally in their teaching and in their leadership responsibilities. We need women with the gift of discernment who can view the trends in the world and detect those that, however popular, are shallow or dangerous. We need women who can discern those positions that may not be popular at all, but are right. ("Relief Society," 8)

Brethren, remember that the purpose of having women involved in our councils is to get their input on the weightier matters of the Church. And remember that they are eager to support and assist you in accomplishing the Lord's work. I believe their feelings are well represented in this comment from a former stake Relief Society president: "If auxiliary leaders feel that they are heard and that they are seen as legitimate spiritual leaders, they will move heaven and earth for the priesthood leaders under whose direction they serve."

In a general Church council meeting I attended several years ago with the presidencies of the women's auxiliaries, the sisters told me that very few women in the Church express any interest in wanting to hold the priesthood. But they do want to be heard and valued, and they want to make meaningful contributions to the stakes and wards in which they live. They want to serve the members and the Lord and to help accomplish the mission of the Church.

An illustration of the importance of a woman's perspective came in one such meeting when we were talking about the worthiness of youth to serve missions. President Elaine Jack, then serving as the Relief Society general president, said, "You know, Elder Ballard, the sisters of the Church may have some good suggestions on how to better prepare the youth for missions if they were just asked. After all, you know, we are their mothers!" The sisters' suggestions can help equally regarding temple attendance and a host of other matters with which priesthood leaders may be struggling.

Again, brethren, please be sure you are seeking the vital input of the sisters in your council meetings. Encourage all council members to share their suggestions and ideas about how the stake or ward can be more effective in proclaiming the gospel, perfecting the Saints, and redeeming the dead.

To be most effective, women need to learn to work effectively with and under the direction of the priesthood. Sisters, be prepared both mentally and spiritually to discuss the needs of those who fall within your stewardship. Be bold. Be assertive. Feel confident about raising weighty issues and concerns. You have as much right to input and inspiration as any other council member. The priesthood leader to whom you report will be strengthened more than you can imagine if he hears what you have to say. You will in many cases view the needs and concerns of women, youth, children, and families with greater empathy and insight than will your priesthood leaders. Prayerfully identify concerns and suggest solutions. Then, with other leaders, be willing to follow and support the counsel of those who hold the priesthood keys of administration in your area. Everyone prospers, at all levels of Church government, by following and supporting those who hold the keys. Both the sisters and the brethren need to understand and practice good judgment and balance in counseling with our councils.

President Howard W. Hunter often spoke about the strength and power that results when men and women combine their strengths, faith, and testimony, and when they work together for the benefit of those whom they serve. He said that "we, his servants all across the Church, need you, the women of the Church, to stand with us and for us in stemming the tide of evil that threatens to engulf us" ("To the Women of the Church," 96).

Perhaps we might look at the respective contributions of men and women in this way: You have no doubt visited the ophthalmologist for an eye exam. In the process of determining a patient's correct vision, the doctor will typically test the patient's eyesight by asking him or her to look through a variety of settings on a machine, some of which are blurry. Not infrequently, the doctor will find that the patient has one eye that is weaker than the other. Only when he can determine the exact prescription for both eyes can a patient's vision be corrected precisely.

In much the same way, men and women express themselves differently and tend to have different skills, talents, and points of view. When either viewpoint is taken in isolation, the resulting image may be blurry, one-dimensional, or otherwise distorted. It is only when both perspectives come together that the picture is balanced and complete. Men and women are equally valuable in the ongoing work of the gospel kingdom.

CHAPTER 5

WARD AND BRANCH COUNCILS

A few years ago Fawn and her mother moved into a new ward. Fawn was a loving, faithful woman who had done a magnificent job rearing a righteous family as a single mother. But now she faced an uphill struggle against an enemy that she probably couldn't defeat: cancer. At the time she moved into her new ward, she could do very little for herself. Her mother tried to care for her, but age and health prevented her from doing everything that needed to be done. Help was needed, but their financial resources were limited. As Fawn's condition progressively deteriorated, the family's situation became critical.

About the time Fawn and her mother moved in, members of the ward council in her new ward were in the process of reevaluating their effectiveness as a council. "We realized that we had been spending most of our time on correlating activities, calendaring, and receiving home teaching and visiting teaching reports," said their bishop. "We realized that we needed to spend more time discussing how we could bring the blessings of the gospel into the lives of our members."

As the ward council became aware of Fawn and the issues

confronting her, the Spirit moved upon council members collectively and individually. "This seemed to be a perfect opportunity to put into practice the things we had been learning about ministering through councils," the bishop said. "Instead of being mentioned in passing, Fawn's situation became a primary focus of council discussions. We felt as a ward council that we could offer the assistance that was needed to help her as she faced the daily challenges of living with cancer."

During their meetings, council members occasionally referred to the Savior's teachings in the twenty-fifth chapter of Matthew:

> When the Son of man shall come in his glory, and all the holy angels with him, then shall he sit upon the throne of his glory:
>
> And before him shall be gathered all nations: and he shall separate them one from another, as a shepherd divideth his sheep from the goats:
>
> And he shall set the sheep on his right hand, but the goats on the left.
>
> Then shall the King say unto them on his right hand, Come, ye blessed of my Father, inherit the kingdom prepared for you from the foundation of the world:
>
> For I was an hungred, and ye gave me meat: I was thirsty, and ye gave me drink: I was a stranger, and ye took me in:
>
> Naked, and ye clothed me: I was sick, and ye visited me: I was in prison, and ye came unto me.
>
> Then shall the righteous answer him, saying, Lord, when saw we thee an hungred, and fed thee? or thirsty, and gave thee drink?
>
> When saw we thee a stranger, and took thee in? or naked, and clothed thee?

Or when saw we thee sick, or in prison, and came unto thee?

And the King shall answer and say unto them, Verily I say unto you, Inasmuch as ye have done it unto one of the least of these my brethren, ye have done it unto me. (Matthew 25:31–40)

As a result of counseling with one another, members of the ward council decided that the ward would reach out to Fawn and her mother in significant ways. The Relief Society regularly took meals to the two women. The Young Women wrote cards and notes, and from time to time they cleaned the house and took fresh flowers to them. The Young Men cared for their yard. Priesthood quorums, working in concert with Fawn's home teachers, offered assistance in lifting things around the house, administering the sacrament, and giving blessings.

"This went on for several months, and during that time many of our ward members came to me to express gratitude for the great blessing of helping these two good sisters," the bishop said. "Through them, we all felt the joy that comes from giving compassionate service in the Lord's kingdom."

When Fawn passed away, her mother spoke with great emotion and appreciation of the kind and generous service of ward leaders and members. Among the last thoughts Fawn expressed to the bishop was that she had never been in a ward that had loved her in such a special way—the Lord's way.

The bishop said, "As council members, we were all impressed by the wonderful way the Lord's plan of ministering provides for his children. Under the direction of the Spirit, the council made recommendations on what steps might be taken in order to provide loving service to Fawn. After experiencing the joyful satisfaction that comes from counseling together in such a meaningful way, I don't think any of us who sat in that ward council could ever go back to the calendaring-and-correlating type of council meetings we used to have."

During the past few years, I have become aware of that same scenario being played out over and over again as bishops and ward council members catch the vision of counseling with their councils. There is literally no problem in the family, ward, or stake that cannot be better understood and helped by Church leaders looking for solutions in the Lord's way. When they make wise use of committees and councils, lives are blessed. This is particularly true on the ward or branch level, where leaders are in a position to have daily hands-on influence on the eternal well-being of families and individuals. The auxiliaries are sleeping giants in the great task of perfecting the Saints—particularly when it comes to strengthening the home. While parents have the preeminent responsibility for family leadership and can never be replaced in that role, Church auxiliaries and programs should do much to sustain and strengthen families.

As I mentioned earlier, I served as a bishop twice. In writing this book I have repeatedly reflected back to those days. My ward council members were a real source of help to me. The sisters that led the Relief Society, the Young Women, and the Primary made a lasting impact in the lives of the women, young women, and boys and girls in the ward because of their spiritual strength and deep love for the gospel.

It would be impossible for me to recount the many quiet acts of service these dear sisters rendered to members of the ward. It was not unusual for my counselors and me to visit a sick member of the ward only to learn that the Relief Society had just been there and left the evening meal for the family. Besides the thousands of meals given, I cannot count the number of families who benefited from wise counsel or who were spiritually strengthened by the sisters who just wanted to help. The wonderful work of the women of the Church is vital. Thousands of young people have had testimonies strengthened and encouragement extended by faithful women leaders. For example, I suppose many of us can remember that special Primary teacher or leader who helped us memorize the Articles of Faith. We must appreciate and never overlook the great contribution that comes from the women of the Church, just as we should work always to sustain the priesthood leadership in our wards and stakes.

For the purposes of our discussion, I will briefly review some of the committees and councils that should function at the ward level.

The *ward priesthood executive committee,* commonly referred to as the "PEC," consists of the bishopric, the high priests group leader, the elders quorum president, the ward mission leader, and the Young Men president. The bishop presides and conducts meetings of the committee, and the ward executive secretary and the ward clerk also attend. Please note the absence of the Relief Society president and other sisters from this listing. Although many bishops have been inclined to invite the ward Relief Society president to attend PEC meetings because she is often the best-informed leader in the ward about what's going on in the lives of ward members, this is simply not appropriate. The priesthood executive committee is just that, a committee composed of priesthood leaders.

When the Church correlation program was introduced in 1963, Elder Harold B. Lee explained in general conference that emphasis was to be placed on "the responsibilities of the entire priesthood to 'watch over the Church' as commanded in the early revelations—to be concerned with the whole family as a group and as individuals." He also announced that a "ward Home Teaching committee" was to be established in each ward of the Church, and that its members would "constitute the core of those who now will go out to 'watch over the Church'" ("The Correlation Program," 504-5). This committee later became known as the ward priesthood executive committee (*Priesthood Home Teaching Handbook,* 7).

Because priesthood leaders have a mandate from the Lord to care for all of our Father's children who come under their supervision, it is necessary for them to meet regularly in order to fulfill their special callings. Priesthood leaders need to work to become as informed as the Relief Society sisters are about the critical personal issues affecting ward and quorum members. The PEC meets weekly under the direction of the bishop to consider the spiritual needs of all who reside within ward boundaries. Frequently, delicate matters are discussed that require confidentiality. As with all councils, PEC members should do all they can to protect privacy when giving reports and making assignments.

The *ward welfare committee* includes all of the members of the priesthood executive committee plus the Relief Society presidency. The addition of the Relief Society president is especially important to this committee, as she carries weighty responsibility in visiting members, assessing their needs, and finding ways to resolve those needs as assigned by the bishop.

This committee meets at least monthly under the bishop's direction to consider the temporal needs of ward members. While the bishop alone is responsible for the allocation of welfare funds, the committee plays a significant role in caring for the poor and needy by planning and coordinating the use of other ward resources, including the time, talents, skills, materials, and compassionate service of ward members. Through the priesthood quorums and the Relief Society, the ward welfare committee builds faith and teaches members to live providently, to provide for themselves and their families, and to care for others. Committee members should assist the bishop in administering welfare assistance, ensuring that families understand and are able to apply welfare principles, and helping to find solutions to long-term welfare needs.

The *bishopric youth committee* is to meet on a monthly basis. It consists of the bishopric, an assistant to the priests quorum president, the teachers and deacons quorum presidents, the Young Women class presidents, the Young Men and Young Women presidents, and the chairman of the ward activities committee. While the primary purpose of this committee is to plan and coordinate youth programs, emphasis should remain focused on activation and opportunities for youth to experience service and spiritual growth.

The *ward council* is made up of the priesthood executive committee; the ward Relief Society, Sunday School, Young Men, Young Women, and Primary presidents; and the activities committee chairman. The bishop may invite others to attend as needed. The ward council usually meets monthly, but may meet more often when there are special needs, to review ward progress on a broad range of issues that impact ward members and the community. Any extra meetings should not supersede or displace meetings of the bishopric or the ward priesthood executive committee.

In my view, the ward council meeting is one of the most important meetings in the Church, because priesthood quorum and auxiliary leaders can discuss and plan with the bishopric the work that is to be done during the coming month. Leaders can then personally interface with one another as often as necessary to assist in the accomplishment of the council's goals and objectives. Of all the councils and committees in the Church, I believe that the ward council can have the greatest impact in helping our Father's children. If this book can help bishops and branch presidents understand the power of the ward or branch council and properly use their councils to accomplish the Lord's work, then my efforts in writing the book will have been more than worthwhile.

RESPONSIBILITIES OF WARD COUNCIL MEMBERS

The critical role of the ward council in helping a ward successfully accomplish the mission of the Church cannot be overstated. Just look around the council table; you'll see two leaders who hold priesthood keys (the bishop and the elders quorum president) and others who are called with the responsibility of presidency over their respective organizations. And when you consider the aims and objectives of those organizations, you begin to get a glimpse of the ward council's potential for powerful influence.

The Primary president, for example, brings a very specific focus to the council table. Insofar as her Church service is concerned, her every thought and prayer is on behalf of the children of the ward. The Primary general presidency of the Church has stated: "The purpose of Primary is to teach children the gospel of Jesus Christ and help them learn to live it. The objectives of Primary are to teach children that they are children of God and that Heavenly Father and Jesus Christ love them; help children learn to love Heavenly Father and Jesus Christ; help children prepare to be baptized, to receive the Holy Ghost, and to keep their baptismal covenants; help children grow in their understanding of the gospel plan and provide opportunities for them to live gospel principles; help boys prepare to receive the priesthood and be worthy to use this power to bless and serve others; [and] help girls prepare to be righteous young women, understand the blessings of the priesthood and the temple, and serve others" (*Instructions for Priesthood and Auxiliary Leaders on Primary,* 1). It is easy to see how that focused perspective could be beneficial to the ward council when its members are asked to consider an issue that would impact the children of the ward, or even a specific child or family of children living within the ward, whether member or nonmember.

Others around the ward council table are similarly focused. The Relief Society president is involved and acquainted with every woman in the ward over the age of eighteen. According to the Relief Society general presidency, she represents an organization that has as its purpose "to help women and families come unto Christ and to assist the priesthood quorums in achieving the mission of the Church." Through training and personal revelation, the ward Relief Society president is dedicated to doing all she can to help the sisters build personal testimony, develop and exercise charity, strengthen their families, enjoy a unified sisterhood, and participate fully in the blessings of the temple while working to bless and lift the lives of the individual women in the ward.

The ward Young Women president concentrates her prayerful attention on the young women ages twelve through eighteen. According to the Young Women general presidency, it is her responsibility to "help prepare each young woman to be worthy to make and keep sacred covenants and receive the ordinances of the temple." The powerful and inspiring words of the Young Women theme provide an excellent outline of the perspective the Young Women president brings to the council table: "We are daughters of our Heavenly Father who loves us, and we love him. We will 'stand as witnesses of God at all times and in all things, and in all places . . .' as we strive to live the Young Women Values, which are: faith, divine nature, individual worth, knowledge, choice and accountability, good works, and integrity. We believe as we come to accept and act upon these values, we will be prepared to make and keep sacred covenants, receive the ordinances of the temple, and enjoy the blessings of exaltation" (*Young Women Leadership Handbook*, 4).

Across the ward council table is the Young Men president, whose Church-service attention is focused on the ward's young men ages twelve through eighteen. He and his counselors assist the presidency of the Aaronic Priesthood in the ward (that is, the bishopric) to administer the ward's Aaronic Priesthood program. They also give leadership to the Scouting program. The mission of the Aaronic Priesthood is "to help each young man become converted to the gospel of Jesus Christ and live by its teachings; magnify priesthood callings; give meaningful service; prepare to receive the Melchizedek Priesthood; commit to, worthily prepare for, and serve an honorable full-time mission; [and] live worthy to receive temple covenants and prepare to become a worthy husband and father" (*Aaronic Priesthood Leadership Handbook*, 6).

The Melchizedek Priesthood leaders who belong to the ward council—the high priests group leader and the elders quorum president—are responsible for the spiritual and temporal welfare of the men over whom they preside. Much of the work among the families of the ward that is currently being done by our bishops could appropriately be performed by quorum and group leaders, who are charged to "follow the Savior's example of righteous leadership. . . . When priesthood leaders lead as the Savior did, they should help members develop greater love for God the Father and His Son; develop greater love for others; share the gospel, do temple and family history work, serve without thought of reward, assist the poor and needy, and minister to the lonely and distressed; receive ordinances and make covenants with the Lord that will lead to eternal life; obey the commandments; become more humble, repentant, and forgiving; pray and study the scriptures daily; attend church meetings regularly and partake of the sacrament worthily; achieve spiritual, emotional, and temporal self-reliance; [and] attend the temple regularly" (*Melchizedek Priesthood Leadership Handbook*, 1-2).

Also seated at the council table is the ward mission leader, whose concentration rests on the nonmembers living within the ward boundaries and who has the sacred duty to help ward members fulfill their missionary responsibilities. He coordinates the work with the full-time missionaries and watches over the fellowshipping of new converts. Two other council members are the Sunday School president, who is responsible for all gospel instruction during the Sunday School portion of the consolidated meeting schedule, and the ward activities committee chairman, charged with planning meaningful social activities that are designed to build faith and fellowship among ward members.

Together with the bishopric, these leaders on the ward council are an inspired collection of men and women with a mandate to bless the lives of every person—man or woman, parent or child, member or nonmember—who lives within the ward boundaries. As a result of their individual callings, they are each entitled to divine direction within their respective areas of responsibility. And as fathers and mothers, neighbors and friends, they each have unique insights into the particular needs of the ward and its members.

Using Ward Councils to Bless Individuals and Families

When ward leaders fully utilize the inspired council system and focus the efforts of the quorums and auxiliaries on improving the spiritual and temporal well-being of ward members, miracles happen in the lives of families and individuals. But those miracles can happen only to the extent that we—the men and women who serve in the quorums and auxiliaries of the Church—are prepared to work together to make them happen. We are on the Lord's errand as we serve His children. To that end, I have three specific suggestions that, if followed, can help us all function more effectively as members of Church councils at both the ward and stake levels.

First, focus on fundamentals. Make sure that the doctrine is pure. Remain true to the approved curriculum. Follow the prescribed handbooks, and study and ponder the scriptures individually and as families. In a world that is filled with conflict and confusion, there is peace and safety in revealed truth. One stake presidency of which I'm aware became known for instructing the leaders throughout their stake to use the scriptures as their basic gospel text. They themselves practiced what they preached, always using the scriptures as a basis for their training and teaching. One year as they prepared for ward conferences, they invited the adult members in each ward to submit gospel questions in advance. In the Gospel Doctrine class held during the Sunday School portion of each ward conference, they then led the members through an exercise of locating scriptural passages that answered each question, demonstrating the power of finding answers to personal problems in the revealed word of God.

A bishop I know was concerned about an escalating lack of reverence in his ward, particularly just before sacrament meeting. When a general conference speaker suggested that reverence might be an appropriate topic for a ward council to consider, the bishop was surprised—and enlightened.

"I don't know why, but it had never occurred to me to take this kind of a problem to my ward council," the bishop said. "Hearing this suggestion sort of clicked a light on in my mind."

The bishop read in his copy of the Church's *General Handbook of Instructions* that "sacrament meeting is held for members to partake of the sacrament, worship reverently, and receive gospel instruction" and that bishoprics should "plan all sacrament meetings and conduct them in a reverent and dignified manner" (sec. 2, 5). The handbook also indicated that the ward council is to "review progress" and to counsel together regarding "all ward programs and activities" (sec. 2, 4). As he considered the quality of sacrament meetings in his ward, it was clear to him that reverence in the meetinghouse was an issue that needed some "progress"—and that any plan for improvement would have to include "all ward programs and activities." So on his next ward council meeting agenda, "Reverence" was prominently listed for discussion.

"I quickly discovered that other members of the council shared my concern, and they had some excellent suggestions for improvement," the bishop said. Several of those suggestions became part of the ward's effort to achieve a greater level of reverence, including decisions to provide prelude music played softly by various talented ward members (including youth) for ten minutes prior to the start of sacrament meeting, to have the entire bishopric seated on the stand several minutes before the meeting began, and to assign ushers at the doors to remind members to be reverent as they entered the chapel.

"I am delighted to report that our reverence has greatly improved," the bishop said. "Following the inspired counsel of Church leaders and implementing handbook procedures has made a difference in our ward."

Another bishop asked the members of his ward council for their suggestions on improving reverence in ward meetings. Hesitantly, the Primary president raised her hand. "Well," she said, "one person consistently does a lot of enthusiastic visiting in the chapel just before and after sacrament meeting. It can be pretty distracting."

The bishop hadn't noticed anyone being especially noisy in the chapel, but he said he would talk to the offending party. He asked the sister who it was.

She took a deep breath. "It's you, Bishop," she said. "I know you're just reaching out to people, and we all appreciate your desire to greet everyone who comes to the meeting. But when others see you moving around the chapel talking to people during the prelude music, they figure it's okay for them to do the same thing."

When others in the ward council nodded in agreement, the bishop thanked her and asked for recommendations. The council soon decided that the bishopric, including the bishop, should be in their places on the stand five minutes before sacrament meeting to set an example of reverence in the chapel.

During a follow-up discussion, the council members indicated unanimously that the simple plan had worked and that reverence in sacrament meeting had improved significantly.

In still another ward, the bishopric was concerned about the sudden increase of gang-related activity in their community. In particular, some of the young people in the ward were being approached by persuasive gang leaders. Parents and leaders were alarmed about a social issue which, up to that time, was something they had only heard about on the nightly news. When the topic was raised during a ward council meeting, a healthy and energetic discussion ensued. Over a period of several weeks—during which the Young Men and Young Women leaders fulfilled assignments to learn more about the issue—the council developed a plan of action that included holding special youth firesides, providing training for parents, scheduling interviews with the youth, and implementing a ward-wide effort to better prepare their young people to deal with gang pressure. Though there was no quick fix to the problem, over time all of the youth who had flirted with gang involvement returned to full fellowship in the ward.

Second, focus on people, not programs. While there is a time and place for program coordination and calendaring, too many council meetings begin and end there. Rather than hearing a litany of organizational plans and reports, the council should spend most of its time pursuing such agenda items as the integration of new members, activation of the less active, concerns of the youth, the economic plight of individual members, and the needs of single mothers and widows. When organizational reports are given, they ought to be measured in terms of meeting those kinds of people-related goals.

One bishop reported to me that "the primary focus of our ward council meeting is people. At any given time, we concentrate on a few families that could benefit from a little extra attention, with every organization taking part in the effort."

One family that was part of this effort consisted of two parents, three teenagers (two girls and a boy), and two Primary-age children. Both parents were members of the Church, but the entire family had been less active since they moved into the area seven years earlier. As a result of the ward council's focus on this family, specific initiatives were undertaken in their behalf by the Primary, the Young Women, the Young Men, the Relief Society, the elders quorum, and the bishopric, including visits, telephone calls, special invitations to activities, and a special joint activity for the Young Men and Young Women that was specifically designed around the interests of the two young women in the family and their mother.

"This process continued for about seven months, when the family moved," the bishop told me. "At the time they moved, the father was much more interested in the Church and was preparing himself to baptize his younger children. Both of the young women were active, and one of them was serving in the Beehive class presidency. The family had achieved considerable momentum toward increased Church activity, and I found it a real pleasure to advise their new bishop of the progress they had made."

As a result of these kinds of experiences, the bishop said, "the ward council is continually focused on helping people. The council meeting itself becomes very much a ministering meeting, as opposed to an administrative meeting. All of the ward leaders see their callings, and their relationships to one another, in a different light. They realize that they are servants of the Lord, and that their ministry is something they share and coordinate with other members of the council."

Another bishop shared the following experience, which beautifully illustrates the importance of focusing the ward council's attention on people:

Not too long ago, our stake president asked us to concentrate our efforts as a ward council on at least three families. We were to focus extra attention on those families and to remember them specifically in our prayers. Within a month of our beginning to pray for the families we had selected, the mother of one of the families called and asked for an appointment to talk with me.

That night she came to the bishop's office in the ward building. She was very nervous, and she began to explain that about three weeks earlier she had felt impressed to begin reading the Book of Mormon again. She had joined the Church when she was nineteen, and she and her husband became inactive shortly thereafter. For her to begin reading the Book of Mormon after so many years was an event in and of itself. She wasn't very talkative. I asked her if she knew why she had come to my office.

"I don't know," she replied.

I explained that the reason she was there was that our ward council had been praying for her family consistently for the past month.

"I have felt it," she said softly.

We spoke of her husband, who was not receptive to the Church, and we considered some things we could do to help. The Spirit bore witness to us both that the Lord's hand was in this.

After that interview, things began to happen. There were two children in the family, an eleven-year-old girl and a fourteen-year-old boy, and neither of them had been baptized. We met as a ward council and outlined what the priesthood quorum and each auxiliary organization could do to help the family return to activity. The ward mission leader visited the family and invited them to take the missionary lessons, which they did. The

Primary presidency visited the daughter and invited her to Primary, and the Young Men presidency invited the son to attend Young Men activities and classes. The Relief Society and elders quorum presidency and the bishopric all made visits to the family and invited them to participate, as did their new home and visiting teachers. The parents also met with the stake presidency. Through all of these correlated efforts, the family had a series of spiritual experiences that led them back to full activity in the Church.

The culmination of our shared experience with this family occurred in the Arizona Temple, where they were sealed as an eternal family unit. Many members of our ward council were present for this sacred event, and many humble tears of appreciation were shed by council members who saw firsthand what following the Lord's program could mean in the lives of His children.

The bishop concluded that "focusing on this family's needs as a ward council accomplished, in my estimation, two things: it opened their hearts to receive the gospel into their lives once more, and it also opened our hearts to receive them. When they started coming back to church, ward council members made special efforts to fellowship them because they felt that their prayers were at least in part responsible for the family's return."

Third, councils are for counsel and the exchange of ideas, not just reports and lectures. Free and open discussion is critical if we are going to take advantage of the experiences, insights, and inspiration of each individual council member. Leaders should work to establish a climate conducive to such openness, where every person and group is important and every opinion is valuable. And don't forget: in our council meetings, the presiding officers should listen at least as much as they speak—and sometimes more.

When a single mother approached her bishop about the possibility of providing a "big brother" for her seven-year-old son, the bishop took the request to the ward council.

"The boy is very energetic," the bishop explained in the council meeting. "He is a challenge for his Primary teacher and for his teacher at school. His mother thinks it would be good for him to have an adult male in his life who could spend time with him in order to do 'boy' things with him and to be a positive male influence."

After the bishop turned the matter over to the ward council for discussion, he silently considered the things that were being said. Some good ideas were expressed, but the meeting turned around when a counselor in the elders quorum presidency, who was attending the meeting as a substitute because the elders quorum president was out of town, raised his hand to speak.

"I was once in the same position that boy is in now," the counselor said. "My mother was a single parent when I was young, and she wanted me to have a 'big brother.'" He then explained that his best experiences occurred when one of those "big brothers" brought along a young son or another boy who was his age, and he urged the council to find for the young man in their ward a "big brother" situation that could include a "little brother" as well.

"What a blessing it was for our ward council to have that insight from this good man," the bishop said. "We concluded that portion of the council meeting with some assignments that reflected the counselor's recommendations. An appropriate big brother–little brother combination was found. How grateful I was that our ward council was functioning in the way that we have been encouraged to function, with free and open discussion of all relevant issues by all of those attending."

A letter which President Gordon B. Hinckley received from a single mother and shared in the October 1996 general conference reflects the positive results of ward leaders working together to care for families and individuals:

> Although I have been raising our four boys as a single parent, . . . I am not alone. I have a wonderful 'ward family' that has rallied around us. . . .
>
> My Relief Society president has been there for me through my greatest hardships, encouraging my spiritual growth, personal prayer, and temple attendance.
>
> Our bishop has been generous in providing needed food and clothing and has helped send two of the boys to camp. He has had interviews with all of us and given each of us blessings and needed encouragement. He has helped me to budget and do what I can to help my family.
>
> Our home teachers have come regularly and even gave the boys blessings as they started the new school year.
>
> Our stake president and his counselors have checked in on us on a regular basis by taking time to visit with us at church, on the phone, or visiting our home.
>
> This Church is true, and my boys and I are living proof that God loves us and that a 'ward family' can make all the difference.
>
> Our priesthood leaders have been instrumental in keeping the boys active in church and in the Scouting program. [One] is an Eagle Scout and is receiving his fourth palm this week. [Another] is an Eagle with three palms. [A third] has just turned in his Eagle papers this week. The youngest is a Webelos and loves Cub Scouts.
>
> We are always met with loving hearts and warm handshakes. The Christlike attitude of the stake and our

ward has helped us through trials we never imagined possible.

Life has been hard, . . . but we put on the whole armor of God as we kneel in family prayer . . . , asking for help and guidance and sharing thanks for the blessings we have received. I pray daily for the constant companionship of the Holy Ghost to guide me as I raise these boys to be missionaries and encourage them to be true to the gospel and the priesthood they hold.

I am proud to say I am a member of The Church of Jesus Christ of Latter-day Saints. I know this Church is true. I sustain my Church leaders. We are doing well, and I thank everyone for their love, and prayers, and acceptance.

President Hinckley went on to say: "What a great letter that is! How much it says about the way this Church functions and should function throughout the world. I hope that every woman who finds herself in the kind of circumstances in which this woman lives is similarly blessed with an understanding and helpful bishop, with a Relief Society president who knows how to assist her, with home teachers who know where their duty lies and how to fulfill it, and with a host of ward members who are helpful without being intrusive" ("Women of the Church," 68–69).

Of course, the function of councils need not be limited by time and place. Sometimes the most powerful ministering happens outside the office and at times other than the regularly scheduled meeting time. In one ward, the ward welfare committee felt a need to teach preparedness among ward members. So the council planned and executed an elaborate "preparedness fair," including a variety of presentations and workshops, and followed it with ongoing monthly training. Another ward welfare committee pooled their individual expertise to help a family through a financial crisis. They gathered information, studied details of the family's situation, taught principles of self-reliance, and offered a host of suggestions and options that eventually led the family out of financial bondage. In both of these cases, council members extended themselves beyond their scheduled meetings to bless lives.

As mentioned earlier, the sister leaders can bring to the ward council special insights and impressions that will help solve many of the challenges facing the bishop and members of the ward. The Relief Society, Young Women, and Primary meetings and programs will often be the most effective place to begin the fellowshipping process for members of the ward.

Most stake and ward leaders would be willing to make the concentrated effort needed in their callings as council members if only they knew and understood these important concepts. That is why they must be taught, and this instruction must be ongoing. Implementation of these principles must be emphasized repeatedly, modeled consistently, and monitored closely. But once they become internalized by the members of our Church councils and committees, we will begin to harness the extraordinary power the Lord has promised to those who serve together in His way to accomplish His latter-day work.

CHAPTER 6

PRESIDENCIES AND OTHER SMALL COUNCILS

When Ronald Black was called as a bishop, he felt the blessing of the Lord in two immediate ways. While driving home from the stake president's office, where the call had been extended, he felt a profound sense of love for the people he was being called to serve.

"It was incredible," Bishop Black said. "As soon as I drove into our ward boundaries I felt an overwhelming outpouring of love for everyone in the neighborhood—even people I had never met. I think God was giving me a peek at the extent and power of His love for these good people, and it was a remarkable feeling. And the best part of it was, that feeling has stayed with me throughout my ministry here. I find myself driven to do the things I should do as bishop because I truly love the people I serve, and I acknowledge the hand of God in blessing me with that revelation."

According to Bishop Black, the second great blessing from the Lord was the inspiration that led to the calling of his counselors.

"Although I had been a counselor to the previous bishop, I

had no idea how important these two good men would be to me," he said. "Not only do I depend on their advice and support; I have learned that it is difficult for me to function without them. While I hold the spiritual keys in our ward organization, it is clear that the ward operates at its best when the bishopric is 'equally yoked together,' pulling together, working as a team. Whenever I try to go out on my own, the work suffers."

WORKING TOGETHER IN LEADERSHIP

I can relate to Bishop Black's perspective. When I was called to be a bishop the first time, I was only twenty-nine years old. I had been a counselor to the previous bishop, and we had shared some wonderful experiences together. But I was still quite young and had much to learn. I am thankful that God sent to me two counselors who had much to teach me. They were both considerably older than I and had experienced much more of life. I can't even begin to tell you how much I learned from these great and good men as we counseled together during the course of our shared ministry in the bishopric.

And that's just as it should be. A call to serve in a bishopric or presidency is a call to serve in one of the most important councils in the Church. This is where the tone is set for the entire organization over which the council presides. When Christlike love is evident in bishoprics and presidencies, it has a captivating, engaging, *healing* effect on the entire organization. Almost without exception, bishoprics, stake presidencies, and auxiliary presidencies who clearly love and respect one another have an almost magnetic effect on those within their reach. Love is contagious; acceptance is balm to the soul. And when warmth and camaraderie are obvious among members of a presidency, similar feelings typically ripple through the entire congregation. Similarly, when bishoprics and presidencies focus on moving forward the mission of the Church, other Church councils in the various organizations follow their lead in working to proclaim the gospel, perfect the Saints, and redeem the dead.

Great things can happen when members of bishoprics and presidencies work together in a meaningful way. Not too long ago I heard about a Beehive class presidency in a small Midwestern ward that became discouraged and concerned because so many girls in their age group had moved away. With the help of their teacher and the encouragement of the second counselor in the bishopric, they decided to take action. They invited their class to devote their fast the next fast Sunday to asking the Lord to send new families with Beehive-age girls to their ward.

Everyone in the class participated. Just two weeks later, a girl who was soon to turn twelve moved into the ward. She had been apprehensive about finding new friends in the ward, and she was greatly relieved to find a group of girls who were ready to welcome her with open arms because they saw her coming as an answer to their prayers. A few weeks later, another girl of Beehive age moved in, and the following month, a third. At an early age these wonderful young women experienced the power that comes when both the leaders and the members of a Church organization focus their faith and prayers toward a common goal. And as this story demonstrates, it is the presidency of the organization that establishes the vision for others to follow.

To some, it may sound unusual or even incorrect to refer to a presidency or bishopric as a council. But that's really what it is—or at least that's what it ought to be. Although the stake president, elders quorum president, or bishop holds priesthood keys and is clearly identified as the person who should make the final decision in all matters, that doesn't mean that he has to have all of the ideas. The same is true of auxiliary presidents, who don't hold priesthood keys but who assume a similar responsibility of leadership within their respective organizations. Wise presidents or bishops will invite their counselors to participate and speak openly. Wise counselors will understand that there are times when they must speak and times when they must support the presidential mantle, which is distinct from any other. Under the direction of the bishop or president, bishopric and presidency meetings (or, in the case of high priests groups, group leadership meetings) should be characterized by free and open discussion of important issues facing the organization. The input of counselors should also be solicited and should be carefully and prayerfully considered before final decisions are made.

Calling Strong Counselors

To bishops and presidents who have a sincere desire to lead their organizations in righteously accomplishing the spiritual and temporal purposes of the Lord, I would offer this suggestion: whenever you are prayerfully considering the call of a new counselor, make sure you look for people who are strong where you feel you are weak. This means you need to have a pretty good understanding of your own strengths and weaknesses as well as the relative abilities—and inabilities—of those whom you are considering to serve with you. A president who is a marvelous motivator but a weak administrator should look for counselors who have strong administrative skills. Similarly, a bishop who is great with Primary children may need a little help from counselors who are more effective than he is at working with the Aaronic Priesthood quorums and the Young Women or in working through administrative details. The Apostle Paul wrote to the Saints in Corinth:

> Now there are diversities of gifts, but the same Spirit.
> And there are differences of administrations, but the same Lord.

And there are diversities of operations, but it is the same God which worketh all in all.

But the manifestation of the Spirit is given to every man to profit withal.

For to one is given by the Spirit the word of wisdom; to another the word of knowledge by the same Spirit;

To another faith by the same Spirit; to another the gifts of healing by the same Spirit;

To another the working of miracles; to another prophecy; to another discerning of spirits; to another divers kinds of tongues; to another the interpretation of tongues:

But all these worketh that one and the selfsame Spirit, dividing to every man severally as he will. (1 Corinthians 12:4-11)

Wise presidents and bishops will recognize and appreciate such diversities of gifts. They will seek to enlarge the capacity of their presidencies, bishoprics, and other councils by involving those who bring gifts and abilities that are not already found therein. As noted earlier, Paul went on to compare the organization of the Church (or, in our context, the Church council) to our physical bodies, stressing the importance of each part to the successful operation of the whole:

But now hath God set the members every one of them in the body, as it hath pleased him. . . .

And the eye cannot say unto the hand, I have no need of thee: nor again the head to the feet, I have no need of you.

Nay, much more those members of the body, which seem to be more feeble, are necessary. . . .

Now ye are the body of Christ, and members in particular.

And God hath set some in the church, first apostles, secondarily prophets, thirdly teachers, after that miracles, then gifts of healings, helps, governments, diversities of tongues.

Are all apostles? are all prophets? are all teachers? are all workers of miracles?

Have all the gifts of healing? do all speak with tongues? do all interpret?

But covet earnestly the best gifts. (1 Corinthians 12:18, 21–22; 27–31)

Bishops and presidents would do well to "covet earnestly the best gifts" among those whom they call to serve at their side. Don't be intimidated by those whose native talents and capabilities may be more visible—and may therefore seem more valuable—than your own. Every person has a significant contribution to make. *Every* person.

When I was called to serve as president of the Canada Toronto Mission, I was overwhelmed by the exciting challenge that lay before me. Still, I was absolutely confident that God could make me equal to the task—except in one respect. When I first entered Canada, I really knew very little about Toronto, and even less about the Church in Ontario. I didn't know where things were, I didn't know where the Church was strong or weak, and I had no idea about the people who could be of most help to me in my ministry there. I am grateful that the Lord inspired me to call as my counselors two extraordinary men who were both mature priesthood leaders with a keen sense of the people and the history that is so important to Latter-day Saints in the Toronto area. These two counselors and their insights and knowledge were invaluable to me and to the work we were performing in Canada. They knew things that I could never have known, and they helped me in ways that I appreciate more with each passing year because they brought into our mission presidency background and experience that I lacked. As a result, our presidency—and, not coincidentally, my ministry as a mission president—was better, fuller, and more complete.

My experiences as a bishop and as a mission president taught me that the role of counselors is vital to the success of any presidency or bishopric. Once again, Moses provides a meaningful illustration of the principle we're discussing. During a great battle between the people of Amalek and the children of Israel, Moses stood on a hill with the rod of God in his hand. "And it came to pass, when Moses held up his hand, that Israel prevailed: and when he let down his hand, Amalek prevailed. But Moses' hands were heavy; and they took a stone, and put it under him, and he sat thereon; and Aaron and Hur stayed up his hands, the one on the one side, and the other on the other side; and his hands were steady until the going down of the sun" (Exodus 17:11-12).

In a very real sense, counselors to priesthood and auxiliary leaders serve the same function as Aaron and Hur did for Moses: they support, they sustain, and they keep things steady.

HOLDING EFFECTIVE PRESIDENCY AND BISHOPRIC MEETINGS

To help bishoprics and presidencies accomplish the mission of the Church through their executive meetings, I would offer several suggestions. First, as we noted in Chapter 3, stay focused on the things that matter most. It's easy to get sidetracked by administrative details, but Church leaders will be much more effective if they will give their primary emphasis to meeting the needs of individuals and families. Specifically, presidencies and bishoprics should concentrate on bringing souls to Christ through the ordinances and covenants of the gospel. President Boyd K. Packer has said:

We urge you now to concentrate on the mission of the Church rather than to merely manage organizations and programs. . . .

You may wonder how to proceed to implement the mission of the Church in the lives of your members. Where should you focus your attention and energy? . . .

We are to bring to pass the immortality and eternal life of man by concentrating on *ordinances* and on the *covenants* associated with them. . . .

If we will set . . . our mind to the words *ordinance* and *covenant,* and then look up, light will come through. Then you will know how to fix your position and plot your course. . . .

A good and useful and true test of every major decision made by a leader in the Church is whether a given course leads toward or away from the making and keeping of covenants. . . .

We would do well to see that in administering the organizations of the Church, *all roads lead to the temple.* For it is there that we are prepared in all things to qualify us to enter the presence of the Lord. (Address at Regional Representatives' seminar, 3 Apr. 1987, 3-5; emphasis added)

To accomplish that, you should see that the written agenda for each executive meeting, especially on the ward or quorum level, focuses mainly on people rather than programs—and then make sure that you follow your agenda. The purposes of the meeting should be clear, and it should start and end on time. If you are the presiding officer, allow sufficient time to discuss people's needs. As you consider each name on the agenda, invite your counselors to suggest ideas and recommendations for helping the person advance through the ordinances and covenants of the gospel. After listening carefully and sincerely to these recommendations, make a decision or assignment that will result in a specific, measurable course of action. It's important to make such decisions prayerfully, and it's also important that you and your counselors are in agreement on the action to be taken.

Of course, it's not enough to simply *talk* about what should be done. We must also *do* it. Thus all decisions and assignments should be recorded and should be communicated to those who need to be involved in carrying them out. One member of the bishopric or presidency should be asked to take responsibility for each assignment, and he or she should be asked to "return and report" on an agreed-upon date. (An ongoing assignment list, maintained by your secretary or executive secretary, will enable you to call for a brief accounting on all assignments as their due dates are reached.) Also, when an assignment is delegated, it should normally be communicated in terms of "what" rather than "how"; that is, the person receiving it should be accountable for the result to be achieved rather than the specific methods to be used. This allows him or her to seek inspiration and to exercise creativity, within established Church policies and procedures, in accomplishing the task that has been delegated.

OTHER COUNCILS IN THE CHURCH

The structure of the Church includes other important councils. Like bishoprics and presidencies, they are generally smaller than stake and ward councils, but they too have been charged to help accomplish the Lord's work. Among these are auxiliary boards, quorum and group committees, priesthood interviews, and home teaching interviews. The principles and suggestions we've discussed in relation to bishoprics and presidencies also apply in many ways to these other councils.

For example, the bishop interviews the elders quorum president and the high priests group leader at least quarterly to discuss "the progress of individuals and families in the ward." As they counsel together during these meetings, the bishop "offers ward resources to help priesthood leaders fulfill their responsibilities to teach, watch over, and strengthen fathers, families, and single members. The leaders, in turn, offer quorum or group resources to help the members of the bishopric with their responsibilities" (*Melchizedek Priesthood Leadership Handbook*, 22).

Similarly, quorum and group committees are formed to carry out the threefold mission of the Church. Melchizedek Priesthood leaders are instructed to "organize three committees to help their members proclaim the gospel, perfect the Saints, and redeem the dead. When used properly, these committees can reduce the work load of priesthood leaders and provide meaningful participation for members. . . . A member of the quorum presidency or group leadership supervises each committee" (ibid., 10).

Speaking of the organization of Melchizedek Priesthood quorums, President Stephen L Richards once said:

> Now, brethren of priesthood quorum presidencies: You need those councils, and I have no hesitancy in giving you the assurance, if you will confer in council as you are expected to do, God will give you solutions to the problems that confront you with reference to your quorums. And he will enable you to find ways and means of approaching the men whom you would like to reach to bring them into accord with your quorum, and have them enjoy its spirit. . . . No matter how many committees you appoint, the quorum presidency is responsible for every man in the quorum; and I am sure you cannot be relieved of that responsibility, although you will want the help of all those who may come to your assistance. (In Conference Report, Oct. 1953, 86)

"To Agree upon My Word"

I believe that we sometimes overlook the importance of one kind of priesthood council that has tremendous power to bring individuals and families to Christ: the home teaching interview. It is primarily through these interviews that quorum and group leaders can provide vision and guidance to the priesthood home teaching program, which is "the Lord's way of watching over the Saints. Through home teaching, priesthood brethren are joined in partnership with the Lord in bringing about His purposes" (*Melchizedek Priesthood Leadership Handbook*, 5).

I refer to the home teaching interview as a priesthood council because of its sacred purpose—and because of the Savior's promise that "where two or three are gathered together in my name, there am I in the midst of them." When we read that promise in its scriptural context, we can see that it applies specifically to those who meet together for the purpose of learning what the Lord would have them do: "Again I say unto you, That if two of you shall *agree on earth as touching any thing that they shall ask,* it shall be done for them of my Father which is in heaven. For where two or three are gathered together in my name, there am I in the midst of them" (Matthew 18:19-20; emphasis added). And He made the same promise to His latter-day servants: "Verily, verily, I say unto you, as I said unto my disciples, where two or three are gathered together in my name, *as touching one thing,* behold, there will I be in the midst of them—even so am I in the midst of you" (D&C 6:32; emphasis added).

Counseling together to agree on the Lord's will seems to be an important theme in the scriptures. Consider this revelation given through the Prophet Joseph Smith: "For verily I say, as ye have assembled yourselves together according to the commandment wherewith I commanded you, *and are agreed as touching this one thing,* and have asked the Father in my name, even so ye shall receive" (D&C 42:3; emphasis added). And again: "Hearken, O ye elders of my church whom I have called, behold I give unto you a commandment, that *ye shall assemble yourselves together to agree upon my word;* and by the prayer of your faith ye shall receive my law, that ye may know how to govern my church and have all things right before me" (D&C 41:2–3; emphasis added).

That describes exactly the purpose of the home teaching interview. Its only function is to enable the priesthood leader and the home teacher to prayerfully counsel together and agree on a course of action that will help individual quorum members and their families "come unto Christ, and be perfected in him" (Moroni 10:32). President Ezra Taft Benson said: "We call upon quorum leaders to conduct spiritual monthly home teaching interviews, receive a report on the home teachers' activities, evaluate current needs, make assignments for the coming month, and teach, strengthen, and inspire the home teachers in their sacred callings. Such interviews with home teachers provide a setting for leaders to measure progress and better serve the individuals and members they have been called to serve" ("To the Home Teachers of the Church," 51).

It takes tremendous vision and commitment for Melchizedek Priesthood leaders to fulfill that charge, but it can be done. A young elders quorum president related some of the events that helped him discover the value of home teaching interviews:

When I was first called as the quorum president, I don't think I really had a testimony of home teaching interviews, and I guess my attitude rubbed off on my counselors and the members of the quorum. We didn't schedule the interviews as often as we should have, and when we did try to hold them, most of the home teachers weren't very excited about coming. One of them even asked, "What do we need to talk about that we can't cover in a two-minute phone call?"

In one of my quarterly interviews with the stake president, I mentioned the problem we were having. We talked about it for a while, and he helped me understand why we were having a hard time getting the brethren to show up for home teaching interviews. He had me read a verse in the Doctrine and Covenants that said a priesthood leader's duty is to "sit in council" with his quorum members and "teach them according to the covenants" (D&C 107:89). Then he explained that the real agenda of the home teaching interview is to agree on the "next step" to help each quorum member come unto Christ.

He said our presidency would have more success if we would focus every interview on this question: "What does the Lord want us to do in the next thirty days to help each brother and his family move closer to the ordinances and covenants of the temple?" He also suggested some ways to follow up on the decisions and assignments we make in the interviews.

In our next quorum presidency meeting, I talked with my counselors about my discussion with the stake president. We agreed to hold more regular interviews and to try a different approach. I remember that we had to reorganize three or four home teaching assignments that night, and we were a lot more careful about it than usual. When we prayed about our decisions at the end of the meeting, we all felt good about them. I think it was during that presidency meeting that things really started to change in our quorum.

That Sunday, instead of just handing out the new assignments like we usually did, we interviewed every home teacher who had a new assignment and explained what we were trying to accomplish. Some of them were more enthusiastic than others, but I especially remember the interview I had with Gary Martinez. Gary was the one who thought we should do our interviews over the phone, so I was a little nervous about asking him to meet with me, but he didn't seem to mind.

After we knelt down and had a prayer, I spent a few minutes telling Gary about his new families. One of the men on the list was Ed Barker, who had just moved into the ward a few weeks before. I told Gary that we were "calling him on a mission" to help Ed become an elder and take his family to the temple. I told him that my counselors and I had prayed about it, and we felt that he was the man the Lord wanted as the home teacher for that family. Gary said he would do his best, and he seemed to mean it. I asked him if he would come for a home teaching interview every month so we could talk about ways to reach our goal with Ed. He smiled when I said that, but he agreed to come.

One of the reasons we assigned Gary as Ed's home teacher was that they both liked to work on cars, so it was pretty easy for Gary to spend time at Ed's house. In our interviews, Gary and I talked about the "next step" to help the Barkers get to the temple, and I could see he was taking his "mission call" seriously. Our first step, with a lot of help from the Primary presidency, was getting Ed's nine-year-old boy into the Cub Scout program. After that, Gary got Ed and his wife, Julie, to come to church a couple of times. One month he got Ed to say a prayer, and a few weeks later the Barkers came to his house for a family home evening. I always wrote down the goal we agreed on, and in the next interview Gary told me whether he was able to accomplish it. Most of the time he was successful, but not every time.

About seven or eight months after Gary started, and after a discussion I had with the bishop, I felt it was time for Ed to be invited to prepare himself and his family to go to the temple. I remember the interview when Gary and I talked about that. He looked really serious and seemed a little worried, but he said he would do it. We knelt and prayed about it, and the Spirit was really strong. I told him that the whole ward council would be praying for him and the Barkers that month, which we did.

Ed and Julie agreed to attend our temple preparation seminar, and Ed was ordained an elder at the next stake conference. He even asked Gary to ordain him. But the day that meant the most to all of us was the Saturday that Ed and Julie and their son were sealed in the temple for time and all eternity. Ed and Gary are both pretty big men, but they shed a lot of tears when they hugged each other in the sealing room that day.

In our next interview, Gary and I just talked about what had happened over the last year and what it meant to both of us. He told me, "When you asked me to talk with Ed about taking his family to the temple, I was pretty scared. When we prayed about it, I knew it was right—but I also knew I couldn't do it by myself. I really needed the Lord's help. And I think He did help me. While I was sitting in the sealing room watching the Barkers, I suddenly realized that I had been an instrument in His hands to help bring them to the Savior and the temple. It was just like we talked about in our interviews. Thanks for giving me the chance to do this. It's been one of the best experiences of my life."

Since then, I've never had any trouble getting Gary to come to home teaching interviews. In fact, he's one of the most faithful home teachers in our quorum—and so is Ed.

President James E. Faust has said: "We must do all in our power to ensure that no member of the Church departs this earth without having received the necessary ordinances and covenants of the temple. . . . As we keep our temple covenants, we place the Savior at the center of our lives, develop greater love for others, receive protection from evil influences, and obtain spiritual strength, happiness, peace of mind, and eternal life" (address at Regional Representatives' seminar, 1 Apr. 1988; quoted in *Church News*, 9 Apr. 1988, 5).

Every kind of Church council, whether large or small, is truly vital to this sacred work of bringing souls to the Lord. May He bless each of us as we fulfill our stewardships in His latter-day kingdom, acting under the direction of His Spirit and implementing the divine pattern He has revealed through His prophets.

CHAPTER 7

DISCIPLINARY COUNCILS

T he longer I live, the more profoundly grateful I am that the Lord has given us a plan to help us grow and progress. As part of this plan, He has given guidance on how we can overcome serious error and sin. His desire is that all of His children return to Him, that all partake of the precious fruit of eternal life (see Ezekiel 18:21-23).

In God's mercy to His children, His plan provides every opportunity for those who fall into transgression to find forgiveness. The repentance process isn't always easy; in many cases it can be accomplished only through official Church discipline. And so God has inspired the establishment of another important Church council: the disciplinary council. For the next few pages I would like to discuss this remarkable tool of love. This is not intended as a complete overview of disciplinary councils, but rather a collection of feelings, impressions, and counsel about this sacred subject. Priesthood leaders are referred to the *General Handbook of Instructions* for a thorough outline of disciplinary policy and procedure.

Both the Lord and those who represent Him in His Church

stand ready with open arms to welcome back all who stray. The First Presidency has extended this special invitation:

> In deep sincerity we express our love and gratitude for our brethren and sisters everywhere. We are aware of some who are inactive, of others who have become critical and are prone to find fault, and of those who have been disfellowshipped or excommunicated because of serious transgressions. To all such we reach out in love. We are anxious to forgive. . . . We encourage Church members to forgive those who may have wronged them. To those who have ceased activity and to those who have become critical, we say, "Come back. Come back and feast at the table of the Lord, and taste again the sweet and satisfying fruits of fellowship with the Saints." ("An Invitation to Come Back," 3)

When members need to have certain blessings withheld, the Lord's object is to *teach* as well as to discipline. Ward and stake disciplinary councils held to impose Church disciplinary measures are incomplete until they are followed by councils of reinstatement and reunion. Although the work of these councils is less public and less generally applicable than other stake and ward councils, it is nonetheless significant in the lives of individuals and families within the Church, and it requires some specific and pointed consideration.

I remember that as a child I occasionally came unkempt to the dinner table. My mother wisely sent me out of the room to clean up and then return. My parents would have been pained if I had taken offense and had run off—and I would have been foolish to do so. In the same way, the servants of the Lord occasionally find that they must, in loving concern, send some of Heavenly Father's children out the door so they can return clean once again. The Lord does not want us to "miss supper."

In fact, He has a great feast prepared for those who return clean and pure through the door. He is greatly saddened when anyone decides to be unclean and miss the meal, finds an excuse to take offense, or runs away. He is pleased to extend the chance to start over.

I've known a few rebellious people who disregard the commandments and who transgress God's laws. I've seen their resultant distress and pain. I've also seen their joy when, humbled and fully repentant, they have returned to the Church and have had all of their priesthood and temple blessings restored.

Some time ago I was asked by the First Presidency to visit a man on my way to a stake conference. This man had been excommunicated from the Church, had fully repented, and had been found worthy to be readmitted into the Church by baptism. But baptism alone had not restored his priesthood and temple blessings. That was my assignment, acting on behalf of the Lord at the direction of the President of the Church.

The stake president, the Regional Representative, and I found the man lying in a hospital bed suffering from a disease that left him unable to move or speak. On seeing him, I realized that it would be impossible to conduct the customary interview. Instead, I felt impressed that I should interview his wife, who was there with him. We found a vacant room in the hospital, and I had a wonderful visit with this stalwart woman, the mother of eight. She had stood by her husband, remaining true and faithful through all his struggles and difficulties. Now she, like her husband, greatly desired that he have his blessings restored.

As we walked back into the husband's room, I asked his wife to help me communicate with him. During the two years that his body had deteriorated from disease, he had developed a way to communicate with his eyes. I leaned over his bed and said, "I am Elder Ballard. I have been sent here by the President of the

Church. I am authorized to restore your blessings. Would you like that?" I quickly saw I wouldn't need the help of his wife. Tears filled his eyes and ran down his cheeks in affirmative response.

I placed my hands on his head and, using terminology associated with this ordinance, restored to him the Melchizedek Priesthood. He sobbed—perhaps the first sounds he had made in some time. I restored his office in the priesthood. Then I restored to him, by the power of the priesthood, the holy endowment that he had received when he went through the temple for the first time. Last, I restored what was perhaps most valuable to him—his sealing to his wife and children.

As the blessings concluded, we were all filled with emotion. I looked at his wife and had the impression that I was to bless her also. I said, "Sister, would you like us to give you a blessing?"

"Oh, I would love a blessing, Brother Ballard," she said. "I have not had a blessing in a long time."

I asked her to sit down; then the other priesthood leaders joined me in placing our hands upon her head. But when I tried to bless her, the words would not come. Suddenly, I realized what was blocking the Spirit. We took our hands off her head, and I said, "Brethren, let's move her chair closer to the bed." We pushed her chair over where I could lift her husband's hand and place it on her head. As we proceeded again with the blessing, the words flowed. Blessings were given; conviction and comfort came.

I have since thought what a marvelous lesson that experience teaches us. This man had sinned, and a loving Heavenly Father had required that he repent so he could be worthy to be once again numbered among the Saints. He had subsequently done our Heavenly Father's will; he had turned his life around; he had repented. Now, back in the Church and continuing to progress, he was worthy to have his greatest blessings restored.

And he was able to use his restored priesthood immediately, participating in giving his wife a special priesthood blessing.

DISCIPLINARY OPTIONS

When a bishop (or, in some cases, a stake president) learns of a transgression, usually through the confession of the member involved, he first counsels with the member. When the sin is not grievous, the bishop may decide through inspiration that no disciplinary action is needed. He may continue to give counsel and caution, helping the member resist temptation and avoid further transgression.

Another option the bishop has is to place the member on informal probation, temporarily restricting his privileges as a Church member—such as the right to partake of the sacrament, hold a Church position, or enter the temple. In addition, he may require the member to make specific positive changes in attitude or behavior, read selected scriptures and Church literature, and attend Church meetings. No official record is made or kept of an informal probation. The bishop maintains close contact with the member and may terminate the probation period when he is prompted to do so.

In these cases, informal Church discipline may negate the need for formal disciplinary action and therefore the convening of a formal council. Since repentance and reformation are the primary objectives of most Church disciplinary action, the bishop or stake president may feel that the person has done or is doing everything necessary to repent and that a disciplinary council would serve no useful purpose.

On the other hand, the spirit of inspiration or the seriousness of the transgression may move or require the Church leader to convene a disciplinary council. A disciplinary council is mandatory for certain serious, specified offenses, such as murder and incest, and also for a serious transgression committed by a member holding a prominent position in the Church. In this context, a serious transgression means a major offense against morality, including attempted murder, rape, forcible sexual abuse, intentionally inflicting serious physical injuries on others, adultery, fornication, homosexual relations, child abuse (sexual or physical), spouse abuse, deliberate abandonment of family responsibilities, robbery, burglary, embezzlement, theft, sale of illegal drugs, fraud, perjury, or false swearing.

In the scriptures, the Lord has given direction concerning Church disciplinary councils (see D&C 102). The word *council* in this sense brings to mind a helpful proceeding—one of love and concern, with the salvation and blessing of the transgressor being the foremost consideration.

THE PURPOSE OF DISCIPLINARY COUNCILS

Members sometimes ask why Church disciplinary councils are held. The purpose is threefold: (1) to save the soul of the transgressor; (2) to protect the innocent; and (3) to safeguard the Church's purity, integrity, and good name.

The First Presidency has instructed that disciplinary councils *must* be held in cases of murder, incest, apostasy, or advocating and teaching apostate and anti-Church doctrines. In addition to these cases and those involving a prominent Church leader, a disciplinary council must be held when the transgressor is a predator who may be a threat to other persons, when the person shows a pattern of repeated serious transgressions, or when a serious transgression is widely known.

Although not mandatory for persons not holding a prominent position in the Church, disciplinary councils should also be considered for other Church members who commit serious transgressions such as those listed above.

Disciplinary councils are not called to try civil or criminal cases; in fact, criminal charges may or may not necessitate Church discipline. The decision of a civil court may help determine whether a Church disciplinary council should be convened. However, a civil court's decision does not dictate the decision of a disciplinary council.

Disciplinary councils are not held for such things as failure to pay tithing, to obey the Word of Wisdom, to attend church, or to receive home teachers. They are not held because of business failure or nonpayment of debts. They are not designed to settle disputes among members. Nor are they held for members who demand that their names be removed from Church records, unless a member who has committed a serious transgression is requesting name removal to avoid the possibility of excommunication or disfellowshipment. The removal of a person's name from the records of the Church is a very serious step but is handled as an administrative action.

The bishopric, in consultation with the stake president, has the responsibility and authority to hold disciplinary councils for ward members. However, if excommunication of a Melchizedek Priesthood holder is thought to be likely, the matter is referred to the stake presidency, who, with the assistance of the high council, may convene a stake disciplinary council in behalf of the Melchizedek Priesthood holder.

If a member feels he or she has been treated unfairly by a Church disciplinary council, an appeal can be made. An appeal of a decision of a ward disciplinary council goes to the stake presidency and high council. Any further appeals go to the First Presidency for consideration.

Missions, districts, and branches have jurisdiction similar to that of stakes and wards, with mission presidents having jurisdiction over the missionaries and over branch members in mission districts.

How Disciplinary Councils Function

After appropriate notice and scheduling, a disciplinary council begins with an opening prayer, followed by a statement from the presiding officer or his designated representative regarding the reported misconduct. If the member denies the reported misconduct, the evidence of the misconduct is presented. The member then presents his witnesses and evidence and makes any comments or statements he wants to make regarding his feelings and what steps of repentance, if any, he has taken. After responding to clarifying questions from the council, the member is excused, and the leaders counsel and pray together. Ultimately the decision rests with the presiding officer, who decides through inspiration. Other priesthood leaders involved are asked to sustain the decision, and differences of opinion, if any, are resolved.

The council takes into consideration many factors, such as whether temple or marriage covenants have been violated; whether a position of trust or authority has been abused; the repetition, seriousness, and magnitude of the transgression; the age, maturity, and experience of the transgressor; the interests of innocent victims and innocent family members; the time between transgression and confession; whether or not confession was voluntary; and evidence of repentance.

Those who sit on the council are to keep everything strictly confidential and to handle the matter in a spirit of love. That includes being respectful and dignified throughout the disciplinary process. Can you imagine how it would feel, if you were a repentant person awaiting a final decision from the stake presidency, to hear loud speaking or laughter coming from the high council room? Whether or not such laughter or conversation has anything to do with the situation at hand, it is unbecoming and inappropriate. Remember, the objective of the council is not retribution; it is to help the member make the changes necessary to stand clean before God once more. Those who come before any Church disciplinary council are entitled to be treated with respect and courtesy.

When a member accused of wrongdoing comes before a disciplinary council, the council can reach one of four decisions:

(1) no action, (2) formal probation, (3) disfellowshipment, or (4) excommunication.

Even if a transgression has been committed, the council may decide to take *no action* at that time. (The member would be encouraged to receive further counsel from his or her bishop.)

Formal probation is a temporary state of discipline, imposed as a means to help the member fully repent. The presiding officer of the council specifies conditions under which the probation can be terminated. During the probation, the bishop or stake president keeps in close contact to help the individual progress.

Like formal probation, *disfellowshipment* is usually a temporary form of discipline to aid in the repentance process. Disfellowshipped persons retain membership in the Church. They are encouraged to attend public Church meetings but are not entitled to offer public prayers or give talks. They may not hold a Church position, partake of the sacrament, vote in the sustaining of Church officers, hold a temple recommend, or exercise the priesthood. They may, however, pay tithes and offerings and continue to wear the temple garment if endowed.

Excommunication is the most severe judgment a Church disciplinary council can impose. Excommunicated persons are no longer members of the Church. Therefore, they are denied the privileges of Church membership, including the wearing of the temple garment and the payment of tithes and offerings. They may attend public Church meetings, but, like disfellowshipped persons, they cannot participate. Excommunicated persons are encouraged to repent and to live in such a way that they may eventually qualify to become baptized members once again.

Great consideration is given regarding the confidentiality of the decisions of a Church disciplinary council. No announcement is ever made when a member is placed on formal probation. Decisions to disfellowship or excommunicate are generally not announced publicly unless the transgression is widely known, the transgressor's behavior constitutes a threat to the Church or the community, or an announcement is necessary to dispel rumors. Even when an announcement is made, it is limited to a general statement of the outcome.

FACILITATING CHANGE THROUGH COUNCILS

Church disciplinary action is not intended to be the end of the process—rather, it is designed to be the beginning of a course that will bring the offender back to full fellowship and to the full blessings of the Church. Priesthood leaders try hard to be sensitive to the disciplined person's need for understanding, encouragement, counsel, and assistance. They work to see that he or she has regular visits with his or her bishop; that mature, caring home teachers or others are assigned to help; and that family members receive the attention, counsel, and fellowship they need during the difficult period while the discipline is imposed.

The desired result is that the person will make whatever changes are necessary to return fully and completely and to be able to receive the marvelous blessings of the Church. When the person has progressed to that point, the current bishop or stake president—even if the person is now living in a new ward or stake or if a new bishopric or stake presidency is now serving—has the authority to convene a new disciplinary council to consider taking action to resolve the discipline.

After an excommunicated person has been baptized again, the membership record will show the original baptism and ordinance dates with no reference to the excommunication. In the case of certain offenses, the approval of the First Presidency is required before a person can be readmitted by baptism. A man who previously held the priesthood but was not endowed should generally be ordained to his former priesthood office.

Again, his membership record will show his original ordination date and will contain no reference to the excommunication.

A person who was endowed in the temple before being excommunicated may regain priesthood or temple blessings only through the ordinance of restoration of blessings. This is a special ordinance performed by a General Authority as authorized and directed by the First Presidency. Afterward, a new membership record is created, showing the original dates of baptism, endowment, sealing, and priesthood ordinations. As in the cases mentioned above, no reference to the excommunication is found on the newly created record.

Our Father in Heaven is pleased to have former blessings restored to His sons and daughters when they have demonstrated sincere and complete repentance.

REACHING OUT TO THE PENITENT

The trauma of being disfellowshipped or excommunicated from the Church will likely never be fully understood by those who have never experienced it.

"The shock I felt was terrible," said one man. "But I knew it was the Lord's will. I could feel the spirit of concern among the brethren in the room as I was told the decision of the council. I felt only love and compassion."

Still, the pain was hard to bear. "Left to cope with the anguish and grief inside me," he said, "I cried, I prayed, I lay awake at night afraid that I would lose my wife and children forever. Although I continued to counsel with my bishop, I felt alone, with rebellion in my heart many times and feelings of guilt because of this rebellion.

"As I look back now, working through each personal challenge was terribly difficult but necessary, and the whole process was a great blessing to me. Repentance is something that each individual must find for himself or herself in process of time."

Another who was excommunicated explained his feelings

this way: "Eternal progression is a great blessing. It is like swimming in a river where the goal is the pure headwaters of the river. The important thing about progression is not where you are in the river but that you are swimming upstream. After drifting so far downstream because of sin, it feels good to be free of sin's great weight and to be able to begin swimming toward my spiritual headwaters once again."

Friends and family are vitally important for an individual who is struggling to return to the gospel path. Those who are around such a person must refrain from judging. They must do all they can to show love. The Lord has commanded, "Wherefore, I say unto you, that ye ought to forgive one another; for he that forgiveth not his brother his trespasses standeth condemned before the Lord; for there remaineth in him the greater sin. I, the Lord, will forgive whom I will forgive, but of you it is required to forgive all men" (D&C 64:9–10).

A woman who had been a Relief Society president tells of the love and support she received during a painful period of disfellowshipment: "When the brethren of the bishopric listened to me, I could feel love as I had never felt it before. They all wept with me."

Although she initially felt as if her heart would "break into a million pieces," the next day a comforting spirit returned, and she realized that she would not be abandoned.

One of the most difficult things for her was going to church the next Sunday, even though it was much easier than she had thought. The bishop made a point of welcoming her. With words and without, the bishopric who had participated on the council expressed their concern and love. No one else knew. "There was no sign of disrespect," she said.

As the weeks and months passed, she found that her pain and suffering were actually aiding the cleansing and healing process. In fact, her pain and suffering served a necessary purpose in the process of healing. And the pain that her family experienced was relieved somewhat through the kind and thoughtful attention extended to them by others.

With agony she acknowledges, "Every member of the Church must realize that he or she is capable of sinning. How I have paid for fooling myself about what I was doing!"

PROTECTING OURSELVES FROM SIN

We must constantly guard our thoughts. Serious sin almost always begins with unworthy thoughts. Some years ago at the direction of the First Presidency, I interviewed a man for the restoration of his priesthood and temple blessings. This brother had been excommunicated while serving in an important calling in his ward. While we visited, I asked him, "How did this all happen?"

In very sober terms he said, "It all began when I picked up a pornographic magazine and read it. From this subtle beginning, I was led to more and more erotic things—including R- and X-rated films and videotapes—until I committed adultery with a prostitute."

He continued: "As I look back, I can hardly believe I did those awful things. But I did them, and it all started by reading a pornographic magazine. Brother Ballard, tell the Saints to be careful about what they read and what they see on television, movies, and videos."

Another young man who found himself in much the same circumstance later attributed his return to the Church to several friends and ward members who took him under their collective wing and helped him to feel that his was a soul worth saving. The elders quorum president, in particular, along with his entire family, befriended this man and his wife. They made the distressed couple feel loved, needed, and valued, and helped the man feel welcome at Church.

A sister who was disciplined after years of faithful service and devotion to the Church said: "I had no idea I was capable of committing such a serious transgression. I had assumed that if I *knew* something was wrong, I would never do it. Little did I understand the sometimes strange dynamics of human behavior, or what I was capable of."

Never forget that. Satan is real, and he has the power to "grasp" mortals "with his everlasting chains . . . and [lead] them away carefully down to hell" (2 Nephi 28:19, 21). Ward and stake disciplinary councils are an important part of God's plan to redeem His children from the chains of sin. All who serve on those councils or who work with loved ones who have been disciplined need to remember to love without judging; to be sensitive and thoughtful without prying; to be warm and caring without being condescending; to be forgiving and forgetful. Above all else, we need to remember that the Lord has said, "Behold, he who has repented of his sins, the same is forgiven, and I, the Lord, remember them no more" (D&C 58:42).

Since we have all become spiritually unclean to one degree or another because of sin, and therefore have need of the atoning sacrifice of the Lord Jesus Christ, can we be justified in doing any less?

CHAPTER 8

FAMILY COUNCILS

When a friend of mine became president of a junior college, he moved with his wife and three children to the president's home near the college campus. Without a mortgage payment, he decided that the family could afford to purchase a new car. But instead of engaging himself in the normal process of test-driving cars, negotiating with dealers, and purchasing the car, he elected to use a family council to make the decision.

"He introduced the idea to our family in a home evening," one of his sons recalls. "The three children, all of whom were in elementary school, as well as our mother, were asked for opinions, advice, preferences, and ideas. We came to the conclusion that we didn't have enough information to make a good decision, so we began the process of gathering information about new cars, which we could review together."

My friend brought home brochures, pictures, and even slides of new cars. The children visited the library, combed through magazine and newspaper advertisements, and talked to friends about car preferences. In another home evening, the family shared the information they had gleaned and began to narrow their focus on the model of car they would consider.

Then the family took several trips together to dealerships, where they all piled in for test drives.

Eventually, the family settled on a make and model. But that was only the beginning of the decision-making process. There were still colors and options to consider. And so each family member was given an opportunity to explain preferences as to features, and votes were taken regarding colors and options.

"As it turned out," one son explained, "the majority opinion fell upon a metallic pink car with a powder blue interior. Mom got to pick the type of fabric for the seats, but I think she was outvoted on the color scheme."

Because few auto dealers carry pink cars with powder blue interiors, a special order was placed with the automobile manufacturer in Detroit. While they awaited the arrival of their new car, the family continued to counsel with each other as they planned the vacation they would take to inaugurate their beautiful new pink-and-blue family member. Following the same pattern of gathering information, expressing preferences, and counseling as a family council, they decided on a trip through Yellowstone Park and the Grand Tetons.

"It was a great car and a great trip," one of the children said. "I don't think any of us will ever forget them—or how they came to be."

That these events occurred in 1957 and are still remembered so fondly attests to the potential power of the family council in strengthening family bonds, building family unity, and creating wonderful memories.

Elder L. Tom Perry of the Quorum of the Twelve Apostles explained that the family council meeting is an ideal setting to teach children "how to prepare for their roles as family members and prospective parents." In family councils, he said, mothers and fathers can provide training in such topics as "temple preparation, missionary preparation, home management, family finances, career development, education, community involvement, cultural improvement, acquisition and care of real and personal property, family planning calendars, use of leisure time, and work assignments." He also suggested that before family members come together to discuss matters as a council, parents could profit by holding "a family executive committee meeting to plan family strategy. The executive committee, composed of a husband and wife, would meet together to fully communicate, discuss, plan, and prepare for their leadership role in the family organization" ("'For Whatsoever a Man Soweth, That Shall He Also Reap,'" 9).

Like other councils, the family council can be a positive, causative force in the lives of Church members. It can help bring order to the home, provide a forum for soothing hurt feelings, give parents an important tool with which to combat outside influences, and create an opportunity to teach profound gospel truths. But like other councils, the family council will be effective only to the extent that it is properly formed and implemented. Indeed, the principles that govern family councils are basically the same as the principles that govern Church councils. Their overall objective is identical. We want for our families the same thing Heavenly Father desires for His family: "immortality and eternal life" (Moses 1:39). We want to develop loving relationships that will extend beyond this life.

Some time ago, I found myself surprisingly short of breath after climbing a small hill. Concerned, I visited my doctor, and before I knew it I was lying in a bed in the LDS Hospital in Salt Lake City. My doctor informed me that it would be necessary for me to have open-heart bypass surgery. The surgeon came into my room at 11:00 A.M. and explained what would be involved. As he left my room he said, "Gather your family around you before the operation."

I didn't pay as much attention to that instruction as I should have. When he came back at 2:00 P.M. to see me again, he asked, "Have you arranged to have your family here with you?"

"Well, no," I said. "I haven't."

He looked at me as only a surgeon who understood what I was facing could look at me and repeated his earlier admonition: "Gather your family around you."

It wasn't until that moment that I began to understand that this surgery might be a little more complex than I anticipated. So I called for my family to come and be with me for a special family council, where a very interesting thing occurred. When they were all standing around my hospital bed, I felt an overwhelming desire to give instruction to the children in the event that something should happen to me. The main thing on my mind was that they should take care of their mother, and the second was that they should take care of each other. Nothing in our lives is more important than each other, and we must look for and capture opportunities to counsel together. Because of the wise counsel I received from my friend and surgeon, my family and I shared a binding moment in life that will live as a precious memory for all of us throughout eternity. Regardless of how difficult some challenges may be, we need to work through them with each other.

We read in the revelations, "Behold, mine house is a house of order, saith the Lord God, and not a house of confusion" (D&C 132:8). Further, the Lord instructed His nineteenth-century followers to "organize yourselves; prepare every needful thing; and establish a house, even a house of prayer, a house of fasting, a house of faith, a house of learning, a house of glory, a house of order, a house of God" (D&C 88:119). Although these scriptural verses refer specifically to God's holy temples, the same principles can and should be applied within the walls of our own homes. Family councils, led by righteous, loving parents who are striving to teach their children to love and respect each other, can make a difference in creating a sense of discipline, order, and loving cooperation in the home.

THE PROCLAMATION ON THE FAMILY

In 1995 the First Presidency and the Quorum of the Twelve Apostles issued a significant document called the Proclamation on the Family. Only five times in the history of the Church have the First Presidency and the Quorum of the Twelve Apostles felt it necessary to make a proclamation to the world on any subject, so you can be sure that this eternal organization we call the family is of extraordinary importance in our Heavenly Father's kingdom. Consider once again the words of the document as it pertains to our discussion of Church councils and family councils:

> We, the First Presidency and the Council of the Twelve Apostles of The Church of Jesus Christ of Latter-day Saints, solemnly proclaim that marriage between a man and a woman is ordained of God and that the family is central to the Creator's plan for the eternal destiny of His children.
>
> All human beings—male and female—are created in the image of God. Each is a beloved spirit son or daughter of heavenly parents, and, as such, each has a divine nature and destiny. Gender is an essential characteristic of individual premortal, mortal, and eternal identity and purpose.
>
> In the premortal realm, spirit sons and daughters knew and worshipped God as their Eternal Father and accepted His plan by which His children could obtain a physical body and gain earthly experience to progress toward perfection and ultimately realize his or her divine destiny as an heir of eternal life. The divine plan of happiness enables family relationships to be perpetuated beyond the grave. Sacred ordinances and covenants available in holy temples make it possible for

individuals to return to the presence of God and for families to be united eternally.

The first commandment that God gave to Adam and Eve pertained to their potential for parenthood as husband and wife. We declare that God's commandment for His children to multiply and replenish the earth remains in force. We further declare that God has commanded that the sacred powers of procreation are to be employed only between man and woman, lawfully wedded as husband and wife.

We declare the means by which mortal life is created to be divinely appointed. We affirm the sanctity of life and of its importance in God's eternal plan.

Husband and wife have a solemn responsibility to love and care for each other and for their children. 'Children are an heritage of the Lord' (Psalm 127:3). Parents have a sacred duty to rear their children in love and righteousness, to provide for their physical and spiritual needs, to teach them to love and serve one another, to observe the commandments of God and to be law-abiding citizens wherever they live. Husbands and wives—mothers and fathers—will be held accountable before God for the discharge of these obligations.

The family is ordained of God. Marriage between man and woman is essential to His eternal plan. Children are entitled to birth within the bonds of matrimony, and to be reared by a father and a mother who honor marital vows with complete fidelity. Happiness in family life is most likely to be achieved when founded upon the teachings of the Lord Jesus Christ. Successful marriages and families are established and maintained on principles of faith, prayer, repentance, forgiveness, respect, love, compassion, work, and wholesome recreational activities. By divine design, fathers are to preside over their families in love and righteousness and are responsible to provide the necessities of life and protection for their families. Mothers are primarily responsible for the nurture of their children. In these sacred responsibilities, fathers and mothers are obligated to help one another as equal partners. Disability, death, or other circumstances may necessitate individual adaptation. Extended families should lend support when needed.

We warn that individuals who violate covenants of chastity, who abuse spouse or offspring, or who fail to fulfill family responsibilities will one day stand accountable before God. Further, we warn that the disintegration of the family will bring upon individuals, communities, and nations the calamities foretold by ancient and modern prophets.

We call upon responsible citizens and officers of government everywhere to promote those measures designed to maintain and strengthen the family as the fundamental unit of society.

Can anyone read and consider those words and not sense the unparalleled significance of the home and family in accomplishing God's will in the lives of all of His children? There never was a time when the world was in greater need of the strength and security that is best sown and cultivated within the deep, fertile soil of familial love. And there never was a time when the family was under heavier attack from worldly antagonists bent on extinguishing a powerful source of light against adversarial darkness. In these perilous times, successful families are built with a wide assortment of tools. And one of the most useful tools in the tool box is the family council, both as a regularly scheduled meeting and as special needs arise. It is in our family councils that we plan family activities, share in one another's burdens and joys, and counsel together toward keeping each family member on the right track spiritually.

SHARING BURDENS AND JOYS THROUGH FAMILY COUNCILS

When members of one family began to feel that an unusual amount of contention was invading their home, a family council was called to discuss the situation. "I began by explaining what I had observed and how I felt about it," said the father. "My wife did the same. Then each of our seven children remaining at home, from the oldest to the youngest, had a chance to express his or her feelings."

The mother and father learned that since their two oldest children had left home, one to be married and one to go to college, an unfair burden of responsibility had been unwittingly shifted to the two oldest children remaining at home. The council resulted in a more equitable distribution of responsibility among the children—and a significant reduction in family frustration levels.

A similar thing happened elsewhere for a family of seven children. "As you might expect, with seven children I often used to find myself frustrated by problems that are common to day-to-day living," the mother said. "Occasionally I felt overwhelmed, and then discouragement would set in. Those feelings always passed, but I did wonder if we would ever make any real progress toward becoming the kind of family that we felt we should be."

Then the parents heard one of the Brethren teach that the basic council of the Church is the family council.

"This hit me with great force," the mother said. "After I discussed it with my husband, we decided to try using family councils in our home. We explained it to the children and began holding family councils every Sunday night.

"I have been amazed and delighted by the results," she

continued. "One by one, we have begun to tackle problems we see in our family. We aren't a perfect family by any means, but for the first time I can see that we are starting to make real progress. And when problems do crop up, I just make a note, as other family members do, and we take these notes to the next family council. We discuss them and deal with them there."

Too often family councils are held only when the parents feel there are problems—and when parents think they have all the answers. Just as presidents and bishops in other Church councils err if they believe that it is their responsibility to come up with all of the answers to the problems and concerns facing their respective organizations, parents are missing valuable insight and inspiration if they choose not to give due consideration to the ideas their children bring to the family council. Remember, although children never have the right to be disrespectful to their parents, they are entitled to be heard. They need a calm setting where discussion can take place on rules or principles they do not understand and where they will be listened to. Family councils are ideal forums for effective communication to take place. Family rules and procedures are more likely to be accepted and followed if all family members have been given the opportunity to participate in the discussions and agree to the rules.

One couple was troubled when one of their teenage daughters seemed to be going out of her way to choose friends whose values and standards were different from the values and standards of the family and the Church. They were particularly distressed to see a relationship developing between their daughter and a young man with a questionable reputation. They tried to battle the adversarial influence coming into their daughter's life by imposing a series of new family rules, threats, and disciplinary measures. But these only served to heighten the tension and contention in the home.

At last the parents decided to form a special family council that consisted of them and their oldest daughter, who was a year older than the young woman who was struggling. "Tears flowed from all of us as we shared our love for each other and our fears about the direction in which our second daughter was heading," the father said. "Our oldest daughter gently suggested that we needed to stop criticizing her sister's friendships, thereby driving them—and her—away from our home. She recommended that we create a friendly environment in our home that would encourage our daughter to bring her friends there, where perhaps we could have a positive influence on them."

After much thought, fasting, and prayer, the special family council came up with a plan: they would try to be as positive as they could be and would try to find the good in their daughter's friends. "We wanted to become friends with her friends so that they would not be quite so inclined to encourage her to resist us," the father said. "We also encouraged her to invite her friends to visit at our home often so that we could keep an eye on things while her need to socialize with them was satisfied."

The special family council also decided to invite the full-time missionaries over for dinner more often. "As our daughter came to know and trust the missionaries, it was a natural and logical thing for us to suggest that she invite her friends to take the missionary discussions," the father said. "We complimented her, telling her that she was the only active missionary in our family because she was the only one who had non-LDS friends to whom we could introduce the gospel."

The resulting missionary experiences were mixed. When the missionaries taught the best friend of the couple's daughter, they said it was one of the most spiritual lessons they had ever given. When the missionaries taught the young man, however, the discussions were not well received. But even that had a silver lining as far as the family was concerned. "Within two or three weeks we noticed that this young man stopped coming around and calling," the father said. "Later we found out that he was telling people that our family was too 'Mormon' for him."

These good parents credit their oldest daughter's counsel in that special family council with keeping their family together. "For whatever reason, her input made all the difference," the father said. "How grateful we are that the Spirit of the Lord was able to work through her for the betterment of our family."

And how wise those parents were to pay careful attention to the thoughts and feelings expressed by their daughter in that special family council.

DIFFERENT FAMILIES, DIFFERENT COUNCILS

There are as many different kinds of family councils as there are different kinds of families. Family councils can consist of one parent and one child, one parent and several children, two parents and one child, two parents and several children, or just two parents. Regardless of the size or makeup of the family council, the things that really matter are loving motivations, an atmosphere that encourages free and open discussion, and a willingness to listen to the honest input of all council members—as well as to the whisperings of the Holy Spirit as it comes to confirm truth and direction.

When one older couple found themselves with a rare gift of time to be alone together, they retired to the sun room in their home for a couple of hours of scripture study together. The husband, who was serving at the time as stake president, interrupted their discussion of the book of Matthew to seek his wife's counsel on a stake matter.

"I never discuss personal situations with her, but I felt the need to share with her some global stake concerns regarding the increasing needs of families that are failing," he said. "I have worried about our seeming inability to be effective in drawing on priesthood power to stop this trend. We had been trying to get the priesthood leaders out of their offices and into the homes of the Saints so they could get a firsthand impression of what is going on in the individual families, but we hadn't had much luck. And so I asked my wife, who was serving as our ward Relief Society president, for her perspective."

And what incredible perspective she had. Like most Relief Society presidents, this great woman had spent a considerable amount of time ministering and visiting in the homes of the sisters of the ward. She indicated that her greatest frustration was in not having adequate time to share with priesthood leaders all of the information she gleaned from her personal contacts and from the visiting teaching and compassionate service reports she received.

"The monthly welfare meetings do not suffice," she said. "And although the bishop and I speak frequently, it is usually regarding specific, urgent welfare matters."

As her husband listened to her concerns, he began to sense the power of the Relief Society and the sisters of the Church. And he grew ever more thankful for the blessing of his eternal companion.

"This family council between husband and wife gave us the opportunity to counsel with each other in a meaningful way," the president said. "The Spirit of the Lord was with us, and as a result of our free and open discussion we drew closer to the Lord and closer to each other, and better able to minister in our respective Church callings."

Family councils can be a blessing in the lives of families and individual family members in this life and through the eternities. Through them we can draw closer to our families and closer to God. They also provide a unique opportunity for fathers and mothers to extend their loving influence in important ways. Another father shares the following powerful example of that concept:

Recently my mother suffered a stroke, which paralyzed her left side and rendered her unable to swallow. It looked as though she would quietly pass away the same evening that she had the stroke. Although she had previously given us instructions that no mechanical support systems should be used to keep her alive in such a situation, the doctor counseled with my father and decided to make her last hours more peaceful with the aid of oxygen and an I.V.

At one point during that long night, Mother became conscious for a brief time and held up three fingers, as if she was indicating that she knew that her fourth child was not yet at her bedside. Then she looked steadily into the space above her bed, reached out her arms, and smiled. We had the impression that she saw something that was not visible to us.

Sunrise found her still breathing but in a coma. She continued in that condition through the day, and in the early evening my brother-in-law suggested that we hold a family council. After recognizing my father's authority as the head of our family, he gently suggested that we have a family prayer around Mother's bed. We did so, and immediately Mother awakened. She beckoned to every member of her family—all, including her fourth child, now assembled in the room. One by one, she pulled them close with her useable hand and reverently hugged each one. When she was finished, she lay back down and slipped back into her coma. We gave her a priesthood blessing, asking that she not be concerned about us and releasing her to return to her Heavenly Father.

The next morning found her still on this side of the veil. For the next couple of days, doctors ran tests to determine if there was any possibility of her recovering from the stroke. Eventually we were informed that her condition was irreversible, and that the only thing keeping her alive was the I.V. treatment. It was up to us, the doctor said, to determine the appropriate time to discontinue that treatment.

My father called for another family council. All of the children, their spouses, and my aunt and uncle were there. When we were seated, my eighty-six-year-old father arose and, after an opening prayer, quietly asked for counsel from each person present. I watched my father take charge and lead the council as I had seen him do on many occasions before. He seemed to become stronger as he conducted the business of the council with dignity, respect, and great priesthood power. Eventually we decided that we would wait for two more days before allowing the doctor to discontinue the I.V. treatment. After he expressed his love for Mother and for us, the council was closed with prayer and the influence of the Comforter persisted far into the ensuing hours.

Mother passed away quietly several days later, awakening once to acknowledge her sister and once when my father gave her a blessing. It was as if she lingered until we as a family were settled in our thoughts and united in our direction. That unity and peace came through the priesthood council, a process ordained of God.

As our families share moments such as these, counseling together from a gospel perspective and with the understanding that we are the family of God, we come to know that He loves us. We are precious to Him. He cares. He wants to help us. He wants to give us the support and help that we need in times of crisis. Much of that support and strength comes through counseling with one another.

CHAPTER 9

"LET US REASON TOGETHER"

The bishop had a few minutes between scheduled interviews one Wednesday evening, so he decided to drop in on Mutual opening exercises just to see how things were going. What he saw frustrated and troubled him.

"I couldn't believe it," the bishop said, shaking his head sadly at the memory. "Three of my priests were sitting on the sacrament table, laughing uproariously as the Laurel president stood at the podium trying to open the meeting. A group of Mia Maids were sprawled on the benches on one side of the chapel, carrying on an animated conversation, while a couple of Scouts were arm wrestling on the front pew.

"I looked around to see what the advisers were doing to gain control of the situation, and I could see only two of my Young Women advisers chatting with each other in the back of the chapel, seemingly oblivious to what was going on all around them. Neither the Young Men president nor the Young Women president was in the room at the moment. It was chaos."

The bishop walked to the front of the chapel and restored order. But for the rest of the week, he couldn't get out of his mind the image of those teenagers behaving so disrespectfully in the chapel. The next Sunday in bishopric meeting, he told his counselors about the experience and asked for their advice on what to do. They discussed the issue for a few minutes and decided it would be a good subject to bring before the ward council. So the following week the bishop outlined his concerns before the entire ward council. "The problem as I see it," he said, "is a lack of respect for the chapel as a special place, an important room where each Sunday a sacred ordinance is performed. How do we teach that to our young people in a meaningful way?"

Thick silence hung heavily over the bishop's office. Members of the ward council looked at the bishop expectantly. Finally, the high priests group leader spoke. "What would you have us do, Bishop?" he asked.

"I don't know," the bishop said. "I honestly don't have any answers here. I have some thoughts on the matter, but I'm really interested in hearing what you folks have to say. You are the parents of these young people. You're their leaders and teachers. You know them and love them just as I do. I really want to know what you think. How do we reach them? How do we teach them?"

"Well," the Relief Society president ventured, "if you want to know the truth of the matter, it isn't just the young people who have a problem with this concept. We have adults who don't seem to know how to be reverent in the chapel."

"And it gets even worse out in the cultural hall," the elders quorum president responded. "Have you seen some of the behavior that goes on during men's basketball games? Sometimes I have to remind myself that most of the brethren I'm playing with are returned missionaries, and that we're playing in a dedicated meetinghouse. You'd think that fact alone would prompt us to raise our behavior standards just a little."

"You should try getting everyone's attention at the start of sacrament meeting," one of the bishop's counselors chimed in.

"Last week when I started reading the announcements, my wife said she could barely hear me above all of the commotion in the chapel."

"Okay, so we all agree that we have a problem here," the bishop said. "What do we do about it?"

"There's a song that the children sing in Primary that keeps running through my mind," said the Primary president. "It goes, 'Reverence is more than just quietly sitting: It's thinking of Father above, A feeling I get when I think of his blessings. I'm reverent, for reverence is love. When I'm reverent, it shows in my words and my deeds. The pathway to follow is clear. And when I am reverent, I know in my heart Heavenly Father and Jesus are near'" ("Reverence Is Love," *Children's Songbook*, 31).

"I think that's what we have to teach to our children, our young people, and our adults," the Primary president continued. "This isn't just about being quiet during sacrament meeting. At the heart of this problem is our love and respect for Heavenly Father and the Lord Jesus Christ. Anything we do that doesn't address that issue is going to miss the mark."

"In other words," the Young Men president said, "behaving disrespectfully in the chapel is just an outward manifestation of a much deeper problem that appears to exist throughout our ward. The greater issue here is personal testimony. If we can strengthen the testimonies of ward members, they will naturally be more reverent."

"But we also have to teach them what constitutes appropriate behavior and what doesn't," said the Young Women president. "We can't just assume that if people have strong testimonies they will naturally know how to act in the chapel. I think some of our youth who were behaving inappropriately the other night have pretty strong testimonies; they just don't know that you don't act that way in the chapel. Nobody has taught them otherwise, and so they just act how they see everyone else act."

"I agree with both perspectives," the bishop said. "We need to do a better job of teaching testimony *and* behavior. So . . . how do we do it? Let's start with the concept of teaching reverence, respect, and love for our Heavenly Father and His house. What can we do to help our people become more spiritually devoted and sensitive?"

"Well, I find that the most spiritual high priests are those who attend the temple regularly," said the high priests group leader. "Being in the temple enhances your sensitivity to holy places. So I'd suggest that our approach to adults include a major effort to help people become worthy to hold a current temple recommend and regularly partake of the blessings of temple worship."

"That's a great idea," said the Relief Society president. "But let's not limit the good influence of temple attendance to our adults. I can't remember the last time my teenagers went to the temple to perform baptisms for the dead. If we're trying to teach reverence and respect for the Lord, there's no better place for them to experience that feeling than in the temple."

"That's an excellent suggestion," the bishop said. "I believe our plan should include a component of temple worthiness and worship. Other suggestions?"

"Maybe we ought to consider moving Mutual opening exercises into the Primary room for a while—at least until we get things under control," said the Young Men president. "That way we could send the message to the young people that the kind of behavior that was going on last week in the chapel is unacceptable and will not be tolerated."

"Or maybe we could just do a better job of teaching them how to behave in the chapel," said the Young Women president. "Like the bishop said, there were only two advisers in there during opening exercises, and they weren't doing anything to control the situation. Maybe if we could spend some time in class focusing on what it means to show our love and respect for the

Lord, and then we as advisers commit to being there with them to make sure that they remember whose house we are in, we can help them learn through positive experiences what it means and how it feels when we're meeting in the chapel in a sweet, worshipful way."

"That's great, but once again we're talking about an issue that has broader application than just to our youth," said the ward mission leader. "Remember the family I brought to sacrament meeting a couple of months ago? Two things really bothered them about our meeting: the crying babies and the noise in the chapel from all the conversations between adults, especially in the few minutes before the bishop stood to begin the meeting. So don't assume that adults don't need instruction on how to behave in the chapel."

"Okay—so how do we do that?" the bishop asked.

Once again, the room was silent as ward council members considered the question.

"Perhaps we should ask ourselves what we want to have happen rather than what we want to do," the Young Women president said. "Can we identify our desired end result, and then determine how to achieve it?"

The group considered the question for a moment. "The thing that I want to have happen," said one of the bishop's counselors, "is for people to be able to walk into the chapel at any time and feel calm and peaceful and worshipful."

"I think we want our meetings to be the kind that can make a spiritual difference in people's lives," the Sunday School president said.

"What it comes down to," said the elders quorum president, "is that we want people to be able to come to church and feel the Spirit."

"Beyond that, we want our members to learn how to be open and receptive to that Spirit when it's here," the Primary president added.

"And we want people to experience the feeling of walking humbly before God—both here at church and in their daily lives," said the Relief Society president.

The bishop considered those suggestions and nodded his head in agreement. "Yes, we want all of those things to happen," he said. "And we've got a couple of good ideas about how to make them happen. Are there any other thoughts on the matter?"

The ward mission leader raised his hand sheepishly. "I'm hesitant to say this, but it seems to me that anything we're going to do sort of begins and ends with this group of people in here," he said. "If we leave here and then go out and do a lot of back-slapping and loud visiting in the chapel, or if we whisper to each other on the stand, or if we do things that are counter to creating a respectful, reverent environment in our meeting-house, it won't matter what else we say or do. We've got to be leaders. We've got to be the ones to show respect and reverence, particularly in the chapel, and we've got to help our families be a part of that example.

"Look around you," he continued. "There are eleven families represented here, comprising about fifty or sixty people. Our spouses work in the various organizations of the ward. Our children participate in Young Men, Young Women, and Primary. If we can do a good job of teaching this concept to our own families, we can provide a powerful foundation on which to build our program. And if we expand that to include the families of those who serve with us—our counselors, advisers, and board members—we have an incredible opportunity to make a significant difference in the spiritual life of the members of this ward."

I might add that all too often our members do not show respect for teachers and leaders. Too many personal conversations are carried on in Sunday School classes and during priesthood and Relief Society meetings. The noise and confusion in our chapels prior to sacrament meeting would indicate that we do not have a clear understanding of what reverence is. Reverence may be defined as a profound respect mingled with love and awe. Other words that add to our understanding of reverence include gratitude, honor, veneration, and admiration. The root word *revere* also implies an element of fear. Thus, reverence might be understood to mean an attitude of profound respect and love and a desire to honor and show gratitude, coupled with a fear of offending God. It would be a marvelous thing if we could come into the chapel and prepare for sacrament meeting by having a few minutes of quiet time to ponder about the gifts and blessings we have received. These include gifts of peace, forgiveness, love, mercy, and understanding, and the greatest gift of all, that of eternal life, which is made possible through the life and sacrifice of Jesus Christ. Do you have any idea what discoveries we might make, what lessons we might learn, if we took five or ten minutes before each sacrament meeting to listen to the softly played prelude music and to ponder about our lives and about Him whom we have come to worship?

But let's return to the ward council meeting. The bishop looked at the men and women seated around him. He paused for a moment, considering the counsel of his ward council. "Thank you, brothers and sisters," he said at last, smiling. "You have presented some excellent thoughts about what we want to have happen and what we need to do to make it happen. I feel especially good about building our program on temple worthiness and worship. I believe that that is precisely the focus the Lord would have us maintain. I also like the idea of teaching reverence and respect by precept and by example, and I am fully in line with the suggestion that we and our families can be crucial to the success of our efforts. That's the direction in which we need to go. Now, let's take the next few minutes to develop some specific plans and suggestions. . . ."

Does this sound familiar? I hope it does. This is the way a

local Church council should function, with visionary leadership and free and open participation from all in attendance. Please notice how—

- The problem is clearly outlined and articulated, but the council isn't allowed to dwell on negativity.

- The council leader controls the flow of the discussion without dominating it. He asks questions and calls for opinions, and then he listens.

- Council members speak from their own perspective as individuals and not just as representatives of their respective organizations (such as when the Relief Society president urged baptisms for the dead on behalf of her teenage children).

- Attention is focused on "what we want to have happen" rather than "what we want to do."

- In its deliberations, the council never strays far from the mission of the Church: bringing souls to Christ through proclaiming the gospel, perfecting the Saints, and redeeming the dead.

- Council members aren't allowed to forget the importance of their individual influence and example.

- Input is solicited from everyone, but final decisions are left to the council leader, who relies upon inspiration more than personal opinion in guiding the decisions of the council.

COUNSELING WITH OUR COUNCILS

Counseling with our councils in this manner should extend far beyond stake presidencies, bishoprics, and stake and ward councils. It can also help individual families, priesthood quorums, and auxiliary organizations accomplish their respective missions and goals. The council system can help the leadership of high priests groups, the presidencies of elders quorums, and quorum and group committees fulfill their important responsibilities. Young Men leaders will discover that councils such as the ward and stake Young Men presidencies, Aaronic Priesthood committees, Aaronic Priesthood–Young Women committees, bishopric youth committees, and quorum presidencies and committees will help accomplish the mission of the Aaronic Priesthood. For ward and stake Relief Society leaders, presidency and board councils can be important in helping them fulfill the purposes and goals of the Relief Society. Stake and ward Young Women presidencies, Aaronic Priesthood–Young Women committees, bishopric youth committees, and Young Women class presidencies should counsel together to help young women live lives that reflect the beautiful philosophy espoused by the Young Women theme. Primary presidencies and boards can implement the council system to "teach children the gospel of Jesus Christ and help them learn to live it." Family councils can provide opportunities for open, nonjudgmental communication that enables parents and children to teach and strengthen one another.

These are lofty goals. But then, that's the nature of the work in God's kingdom in these latter days: lofty, far-reaching, eternal. We are working to help our brothers and sisters receive all that our Father in Heaven has to give to His faithful children, including the blessings of the celestial kingdom. Nothing more, nothing less. It is a sacred trust that God has given to all who have been called to positions of authority in His Church. And it is a responsibility that can be accomplished much more effectively and efficiently by using the council system the Lord has inspired Church leaders to implement in all of the organizations of the Church. Governance through councils is more than just a good idea; it is God's plan. It is how we share the burdens of gospel responsibilities. It is how we accomplish the mission of the Church. And it is how God receives His very glory by bringing to pass "the immortality and eternal life of man." As the Lord said through the prophet Isaiah, "Come now, and let us reason together" (Isaiah 1:18).

It is my sincere prayer that we may all find ways to make more effective use of the wondrous power that can be harnessed by counseling with our councils. I testify that it is only in doing so that we can bring the full force of God's revealed plan for gospel governance into our respective ministries, both in our families and in the Church.

Sources Cited

Aaronic Priesthood Leadership Handbook. Salt Lake City: The Church of Jesus Christ of Latter-day Saints, 1991.

Ashton, Marvin J. Address at Regional Representatives' seminar, Salt Lake City, 31 March 1989.

Ballard, M. Russell. *Our Search for Happiness: An Invitation to Understand The Church of Jesus Christ of Latter-day Saints.* Salt Lake City: Deseret Book, 1993.

Benson, Ezra Taft. "Church Government through Councils." *Ensign,* May 1979, 86-89.

——. "I Testify." *Ensign,* November 1988, 86-87.

——. "To the Home Teachers of the Church." *Ensign,* May 1987, 48-51.

Children's Songbook. Salt Lake City: The Church of Jesus Christ of Latter-day Saints, 1989.

Craven, Rulon G. *Called to the Work.* Salt Lake City: Bookcraft, 1985.

Faust, James E. Address at Regional Representatives' seminar, Salt Lake City, 1 April 1988.

——. "Keeping Covenants and Honoring the Priesthood." *Ensign,* November 1993, 36-39.

First Presidency of The Church of Jesus Christ of Latter-day Saints. "An Invitation to Come Back." *Church News,* 22 December 1985, 3.

First Presidency and Quorum of the Twelve Apostles of The Church of Jesus Christ of Latter-day Saints. "The Family: A Proclamation to the World." *Ensign,* November 1995, 102.

General Handbook of Instructions. Salt Lake City: The Church of Jesus Christ of Latter-day Saints, 1989.

Himmelfarb, Gertrude. *The De-Moralization of Society: From Victorian Virtues to Modern Values.* New York: Alfred A. Knopf, 1995.

Hinckley, Gordon B. "God Is at the Helm." *Ensign,* May 1994, 53-54, 59-60.

———. "Women of the Church." *Ensign,* November 1996, 67-70.

Hunter, Howard W. "To the Women of the Church." *Ensign,* November 1992, 95-97.

Instructions for Priesthood and Auxiliary Leaders on Primary. Salt Lake City: The Church of Jesus Christ of Latter-day Saints, 1996.

Journal of Discourses. 26 vols. London: Latter-day Saints' Book Depot, 1855-86.

Lee, Harold B. "The Correlation Program." *Improvement Era,* June 1963, 500-505.

Ludlow, Daniel H., ed. *Encyclopedia of Mormonism.* 5 vols. New York: Macmillan, 1992.

McKay, David O. *Gospel Ideals: Selections from the Discourses of David O. McKay.* Salt Lake City: Improvement Era, 1953.

Melchizedek Priesthood Leadership Handbook. Salt Lake City: The Church of Jesus Christ of Latter-day Saints, 1990.

Packer, Boyd K. Address at Regional Representatives' seminar, Salt Lake City, 3 April 1987.

———. "The Relief Society." *Ensign,* November 1978, 7-9.

Perry, L. Tom. "'For Whatsoever a Man Soweth, That Shall He Also Reap.'" *Ensign,* November 1980, 7-9.

Popenoe, David. "A World without Fathers." *Wilson Quarterly,* Spring 1996, 12-29.

Priesthood Home Teaching Handbook. Rev. ed. Salt Lake City: The Church of Jesus Christ of Latter-day Saints, 1967.

Richards, Stephen L. In Conference Report, October 1953, 85-87.

Smith, Joseph. *History of The Church of Jesus Christ of Latter-day Saints.* Edited by B. H. Roberts. 2d ed. rev. 7 vols. Salt Lake City: Deseret Book, 1973.

Smith, Joseph F. In Conference Report, April 1906, 1-8.

Smith, Joseph Fielding. *Doctrines of Salvation: Sermons and Writings of Joseph Fielding Smith*. Compiled by Bruce R. McConkie. 3 vols. Salt Lake City: Bookcraft, 1954–56.

Smith, Lucy Mack. *History of Joseph Smith by His Mother, Lucy Mack Smith*. Edited by Preston Nibley. Salt Lake City: Bookcraft, 1958.

Snow, Eliza R. Address at Relief Society meeting, Ogden, Utah, 14 August 1873. *Woman's Exponent,* 15 September 1873, 62–63.

Taylor, John. *The Gospel Kingdom: Selections from the Writings and Discourses of John Taylor*. Selected by G. Homer Durham. Salt Lake City: Bookcraft, 1943.

Young Women Leadership Handbook. Salt Lake City: The Church of Jesus Christ of Latter-day Saints, 1995.

INDEX

175

and, 59; unity of, 61; women
leaders underused in, 92-93;
women want to serve in, 94, 116;
critical role of ward council in,
103
Ward activities committee(s): role
of, 12, 132; concerned with
planning activities, 106; and
meeting agendas, 124
Ward council(s): address in general
conference regarding, 3-4; as
resource, 6; increase effectiveness
of, 14; and fellowshipping, 18;
freedom and, 25; role of women
in, 53-54, 92-93; unity of, 61;
confidentiality vital in, 64-65;
effective listening by, 65; ask
meaningful questions in, 65; and
delegation of authority, 66-68;
function of leaders in, 75; focus
of, on mission of Church, 76-77,
83-84, 118, 170; spiritual leaders
in, 92; women leaders underused
in, 92-93; women want to serve
in, 94, 116; share suggestions in,
94; blessings from, 96; service of,
98; members of, 102; critical role
of, 103; inspired, 106; function
effectively, 106; focus on
fundamentals, 106; focus on
people, 109; purpose of, 112,
168, 170; and meeting agendas,
124; and following through on
assignments, 125; vital role of,
132; process of, 168; governance
through, 169. See also Council(s)
Ward home teaching committee,
100
Ward leaders: importance of
listening to, 31; bring people to
Christ, 58; unity of, 61;
confidentiality vital by, 64-65;

effective listening by, 65; ask
meaningful questions, 65;
delegation of authority, 66-68;
and role of counselors, 70, 83,
120; function of, 75; focus of, on
mission of Church, 76-77,
83-84, 118, 170; spiritual, 92;
women leaders underused as,
92-93; women want to serve as,
94, 116; blessings from, 96;
service of, 98; priesthood leaders
lead, 105; should choose
counselors wisely, 120-21; and
meeting agendas, 124
Ward mission leader: resource, 6;
coordinates, 18; and
fellowshipping, 36; and
delegation of authority, 66-68;
and function of leaders, 75; focus
of, on mission of Church, 76-77,
83-84, 118, 170; as spiritual
leader, 92; concerned for
nonmembers, 105; coordinates
with full-time missionaries, 105;
and meeting agendas, 124
Ward priesthood executive
committee (PEC), 100-101;
members of, 100; includes
priesthood leaders only, 100; and
meeting agendas, 124; vital role
of, 132; process of, 168
Ward welfare committee, 15, 101;
unity of, 61; members of, 101;
and temporal needs of members,
101; and meeting agendas, 124;
vital role of, 132; process of, 168
Whitmer, David, as special witness,
37-38
Whitmer, Peter, home of, 37, 39
Witnesses of Book of Mormon,
38-39
Women, 51-54; role of, 51, 53,